Collins

Enhanced English Alive Workbook 8

Kalyan Chattopadhyay

Series Editor
Renu Viswanath

Acknowledgements

The publishers have applied for permission for the following:

'The Great Barrier Reef's Slow Death', published in *https://www.indiatoday.in/education-today/gk-current-affairs/story/great-barrier-reef-larvae-1096762-2017-11-30*, *A Cloud of Trash* by Karanjeet Kaur.
Acknowledgments for the above will be made in the future editions of the book.

Every effort has been made to trace copyright holders and to obtain their permission for the use of copyright material. However, in some instances, we have been unable to trace the owners of the copyright pieces published here. The authors and publishers will gladly receive any information enabling them to rectify any error or omission in subsequent editions.

Cover and Title Page: Created by Toonfantasy

Inside: Page 9: Prospective56; **10:** Godruma; **24:** Nadia Bormotova; **28:** Gulari; **29:** Diane555, Irmun; **33:** Marishka_Yu; **56:** Robuart; **70:** SilkenOne; **88:** TopVectors.

Preface

Enhanced English Alive is a multi-skill course in English that adheres to the guidelines laid down by the **National Education Policy, 2020**. This edition retains the original essence of teaching communicative English using a cross-curricular approach and interactive and experiential teaching and learning methods. It offers high-quality English language materials with a coherent structured approach, effective integration of subject knowledge and life skills.

The series comprises Coursebooks and Workbooks for Foundational Stage (Nursery, LKG, UKG, Classes 1 and 2), Preparatory Stage (Classes 3 to 5), and Middle Stage (Classes 6 to 8). Literature Readers are for the Preparatory and Middle Stages (Classes 3 to 8). Each grade package includes a Teacher's Resource Pack and a Collins DigiSuite.

This series integrates the essence of **NIPUN Bharat** guidelines, which extensively deal with foundational literacy and numeracy. Each book aims to motivate learners to read independently, to improve their vocabulary, to develop their critical thinking and creative skills, as well as to enhance their ability to express themselves both verbally and in writing.

This series takes care of the requirements of **Structured Assessments For Analyzing Learning (SAFAL)**. Research-based activities and projects have been used to instill inquiry-based learning, while comprehension passages have been followed by extrapolative and value-based questions that involve analysis-based learning.

Key features

Coursebooks

Each Coursebook has a wide variety of texts from various genres carefully selected from both Indian and Western literature. The books aim at cross-curricular teaching, covering topics included in the syllabus of other subjects taught in the respective grades. They also inculcate mindfulness in learners in the Foundational and Preparatory stages (Classes 1 to 5), in addition to language skills. A lot of interesting and engaging activities are used as tools to teach language skills. Additionally, in the Middle Stage (Classes 6 to 8), an end-of-year Assessment Paper has been provided.

Workbooks

- **Reading:** Each Workbook has 8 to 11 comprehension passages which include prose and poems. Exercises with a variety of questions follow these passages and aim to provide ample practice for the learners.
- **Vocabulary:** A variety of exercises and activities on vocabulary topics mapped with the corresponding Coursebook are given to reinforce the concepts. Exercises on spelling and pronunciation have also been provided to allow a thorough revision of these linguistic rules.
- **Grammar:** Grammar concepts taught in the Coursebooks are reinforced with summarised explanations and graded exercises.
- **Listening and Speaking:** More innovative activities and communicative tasks have been provided to practice and improve the listening and speaking skills of the learners.
- **Writing:** This well-graded section has a variety of creative-writing exercises.

- **Test papers:** Short assessment papers provide a great opportunity to the learners to revise the concepts of vocabulary, grammar, and writing taught in each unit. Each paper evaluates the concepts covered in a group of chapters.

Literature Readers

The Literature Readers teach critical appreciation of literature through short stories, folktales, fairytales, poems, and extracts from classics from the literature of different ages. The summary of each chapter helps in imbibing the essence of the text. Literary devices are also taught along with a glossary of literary terms.

Teacher's Resource Pack

The Teacher's Resource Pack contain model lesson plans, additional worksheets, and grammar-based projects covering all the pedagogical aspects included in the Coursebooks, along with listening texts and answer keys to all exercises across Coursebooks, Workbooks, Literature Readers, and additional assessment papers.

Detailed Contents

Grammar	Listening	Speaking	Writing
• Subject-verb agreement • Transformation of sentences	• Listening and filling in information	• Debate	• Writing a paragraph
• Non-finite verbs: infinitive, gerund, participle • Prepositions	• Listening and filling in information	• Delivering an extempore speech	• Writing a paragraph expressing an opinion • Writing a biographical note
			• Making a poster
• Tenses: Simple, continuous, perfect, perfect continuous • Question tags	• Listening and answering questions		• Making a brochure
• Kinds of phrases: Noun phrase, prepositional phrase, adjective phrase, adverb phrase		• Reader's theatre: Enacting a play	• Writing a magazine report
• Kinds of clauses: Noun clause, adjective clause, adverb clause • **Punctuation:** Hyphen, dash, ellipsis	• Listening and choosing correct options		• Writing an argumentative essay
			• Writing slogans
• Main and subordinate clauses • Coordinating and subordinating conjunctions	• Listening and matching points	• Asking and answering questions	• Writing an email
			• Sequencing comic strip panels • Writing dialogues for a comic strip
• Direct and indirect speech	• Listening and answering questions	• Delivering an extempore speech	• Writing a diary entry
			• Writing a limerick
• Simple, compound and complex sentences • Conditional clauses	• Listening and filling in information	• Role-play	• Writing a short article • Writing a diary entry
			• Writing an advertisement
• Active and passive voice • Defining and non-defining clauses	• Listening and filling in information	• Interviewing an important person • Justifying a decision and convincing people • **Pronunciation:** Hard and soft *c* sounds	• Writing a letter of complaint • Writing a letter to a newspaper editor
			• Writing text messages and tweets

Contents

1 Partition

READING

Read this poem on human rights.

Human Rights

In a civilised land
That accepts duty to all
Citizens have rights
Some great, some small.

This is how things should be
To those who value
Truth and fairness
And justice and decency.

But those who treasure money
And the power of wealth
Seek to remove such rights
Through deceit and stealth.

They claim that duty
Comes before such rights,
But they accept no obligation
For causing another's plight.

Obligation before rights
Is their loud refrain,
But fulfilling their own duties
Is something they distain.

For rights are for the powerful
Whilst duty is for the poor,
And decency and justice
The country provides no more.

Human rights matter
To ensure justice for all,
For saints and for sinners
For all people great and small.

The alternative is ugly
With justice a forgotten myth,
With power replacing fairness
And a society that is truly sick.

– *David Chalk*

COMPREHENSION

A. Read the lines from the poem and answer the questions.

1. *In a civilised land*
   That accepts duty to all
   Citizens have rights
   Some great, some small.

   a. What does 'that accepts duty to all' mean here?

   ....

   b. Who has rights in a civilised land?

   ....

2. *This is how things should be*
   To those who value
   Truth and fairness
   And justice and decency.

   a. What does 'things' here mean?

   ....

   b. What values should people in a civilised land have?

   ....

B. Think and answer the questions.

1. What kind of life do people have in a civilised country?

   ....

   ....

   ....

2. What happens when powerful leaders and officials value money more than human rights?

3. Explain the last stanza in your own words.

VOCABULARY

A. Here is a list of some basic human rights. Use each in a sentence of your own.

right to life *right to practise religion* *right to freedom*
right to equality before the law *right to freedom of speech*

1.

2.

3.

4.

5.

Abstract Nouns

Abstract nouns are nouns that refer to intangible things like feelings, emotions, actions, ideas, concepts and qualities, which do not have a physical existence. For example:

freedom *arrival* *courage*

B. Add appropriate suffixes to the words and form abstract nouns. You may need to change the spelling slightly in some cases.

Suffixes	Words
-age, -ance, -ion/-tion, -ism, -ity, -ment, -hood, -dom, -ery/ry	develop, merry, hero, absurd, capital, captive, digest, beautify, national, false, slave, snob, free, martyr, short, pilgrim, break, weight, remember, appear

....

....

....

GRAMMAR

Subject-verb Agreement

- In a sentence, the subject must agree with the verb. This is called **subject-verb agreement**.
- The verb form changes according to the form of the subject.
- If the subject is singular, we use a singular verb (with *-s* or *-es* added to the verb in the simple present tense). For example:

  Ramesh goes to the library every day.
- With a plural subject, we use a plural verb, which is the root form of the verb. For example:

  We go to the library every day.

A. Fill in each blank with the correct form of the verb in the tense mentioned.

1. Hard workers always .... (*win*) at the end. (*simple present*)
2. A prize .... (*be*) given to the boy who stood first in the examination. (*simple past*)
3. Dev and Anuj .... (*be*) going to Goa this weekend. (*present continuous*)
4. Watching television .... (*do*) not interest me. (*simple present*)
5. Simple living and high thinking .... (*be*) Gandhiji's philosophy. (*simple past*)
6. Neither of those pairs of spectacles .... (*suit*) your face. (*simple present*)
7. Those clothes .... (*be*) out of fashion. (*simple past*)
8. Rice and curry .... (*be*) my favourite dish. (*simple present*)
9. Neither of us .... (*feel*) that we should sell our old car. (*simple present*)
10. Either Lina or Navit .... (*write*) this mail. (*present perfect*)
11. Both Mukul and Sangeeta .... (*complete*) their work. (*present perfect*)
12. Some people .... (*believe*) that all snakes are poisonous. (*simple present*)

Transformation of Sentences

There are four types of sentences: declarative, interrogative, imperative, and exclamatory sentences. Here are some rules for the **transformation of sentences**.

Declarative to Interrogative

- To change a declarative sentence into interrogative, we place the helping verb before the subject. For example:

  Mukul is drawing pictures. (declarative)

  Is Mukul drawing pictures? (interrogative)

- If there is no helping verb in a declarative sentence, we add *do/does/did*, as appropriate, and the base form of the main verb. For example:

  Anjali lives in Switzerland. (declarative)

  Does Anjali live in Switzerland? (interrogative)

  Navit had an interesting dream last night. (declarative)

  Did Navit have an interesting dream last night? (interrogative)

- We use a *wh-* word at the beginning to ask for information. For example:

  Sarika is from Bhopal. (declarative)

  Where is Sarika from? (interrogative)

  Raman lives with his uncle. (declarative)

  Who does Raman live with? (interrogative)

  Kapil doesn't do his homework regularly. (declarative)

  Why doesn't Kapil do his homework regularly? (interrogative)

Declarative to Imperative

- While a declarative sentence begins with a subject, an imperative sentence begins with a verb or with *do/don't/do not/always/never/please/kindly* followed by a verb. The subject, usually *you*, is understood and hence not mentioned. For example:

  You should learn this poem. (declarative)

  Learn this poem. (imperative)

  You should not disturb me. (declarative)

  Do not/Don't disturb me. (imperative)

  I request you to help me. (declarative)

  Please help me. (imperative)

  You should always follow the rule. (declarative)

  Always follow the rule. (imperative)

Declarative to Exclamatory

- We can change a declarative sentence containing an adjective followed by a noun into an exclamatory sentence by using *what* at the beginning and placing the verb after the noun. For example:

  It is an interesting story. (declarative)

  What an interesting story it is! (exclamatory)

  Lina is a very talented artist. (declarative)

  What a talented artist Lina is! (exclamatory)

- When the adjective/adverb in the declarative sentence is not followed by a noun, we change the sentence into an exclamatory sentence by using *how* before the adjective/adverb. For example:

  Sonakshi is very intelligent. (declarative)

  How intelligent Sonakshi is! (exclamatory)

  Navit is very lazy. (declarative)

  How lazy Navit is! (exclamatory)

  The old man looks extremely weak. (declarative)

  How weak the old man looks! (exclamatory)

Changing Affirmative Sentences into Negative

To change affirmative sentences into negative, we insert *not* before the main verb or its contraction *n't* with the helping verb in declarative and interrogative sentences. For example:

I told you about my trip. (affirmative)

Did I not tell you about my trip?/Didn't I tell you about my trip? (negative)

Did you visit your uncle yesterday? (affirmative)

Did you not visit your uncle yesterday?/Didn't you visit your uncle yesterday? (negative)

Can you lift this box? (affirmative)

Can you not lift this box?/Can't you lift this box? (negative)

B. Change the sentences as directed.

1. You should never tell a lie. (*imperative sentence*)

   ....

2. You spoke very fast. (*negative sentence*)

   ....

3. Does Aman like horror films? (*declarative sentence*)

   ....

4. Lina likes to play video games. (*interrogative sentence*)

   ....

5. It is a fabulous film. (*exclamatory sentence*)

....

6. She is a brilliant student. (*exclamatory sentence*)

....

7. What a beautiful scene it is! (*declarative sentence*)

....

8. You must not switch on the fan. (*imperative sentence*)

....

9. You are very smart. (*exclamatory sentence*)

....

10. He exercises every day. (*negative sentence*)

....

11. How excited Anjali looks! (*declarative sentence*)

....

12. You should write to the principal. (*imperative sentence*)

....

13. It was a marvellous performance. (*exclamatory sentence*)

....

14. I request you to open the door. (*imperative sentence*)

....

LISTENING AND SPEAKING

Listening

A. Listen to a conversation between two friends at school and fill in the blanks.

1. Natasha is talking about a session on ....
2. The session will take place on the school ....
3. The session is being conducted by the Indian Institute of ....
4. The objective of the session is to make students aware of their basic ....
5. If we complain about our rights being violated, the .... system helps us fight injustice.

Speaking

B. Work in groups and hold a debate in class on the topic: *Is protecting individual human rights more important than protecting the rights of the community?*
Each group will take turns to present their arguments and counter-arguments.

WRITING

Write a paragraph highlighting the impact of social media on human rights.

2 A Girl's Incredible Journey from Syria

READING

Read this passage on human rights.

The Universal Declaration of Human Rights

The Universal Declaration of Human Rights (UDHR) was adopted on 10 December 1948. The day is now celebrated as Human Rights Day worldwide. The High Commissioner for Human Rights is the main UN rights official and his/her office plays a major role in coordinating efforts for the yearly observance of Human Rights Day. The day celebrates the work of human rights organisations and the efforts of all those who defend human rights worldwide.

Human Rights Day came into being when the United Nations Assembly adopted the Universal Declaration of Human Rights, which was the first global enactment for human rights. All over the world, many people—among them some renowned and some anonymous—work in groups, organisations or alone to promote human rights and end discrimination of all kinds. Many governmental and non-governmental organisations also actively participate in various activities organised for Human Rights Day so that people everywhere learn about their rights.

The United Nations General Assembly has declared the Universal Declaration of Human Rights as a common standard of achievement for all people and all nations. It states that every individual and every organ of society shall strive to promote respect for these rights and freedoms. It aims to secure the universal and effective recognition and observance of human rights. Human Rights Day promotes and spreads awareness about the following articles under UDHR:

- All human beings are born free and equal in dignity and rights.
- Everyone is entitled to all the rights and freedoms set forth in this Declaration, without distinction of any kind, such as race, colour, sex, language, religion, political or other opinion, national or social origin, property, birth, or other status.
- Everyone has the right to life, liberty, and security of person.

- No one shall be held in slavery or servitude; slavery and the slave trade shall be prohibited in all their forms.
- No one shall be subjected to torture or to cruel, inhuman or degrading treatment or punishment.
- Everyone has the right to recognition everywhere as a person before the law.
- All are equal before the law and are entitled without any discrimination to equal protection of the law.
- Everyone has the right to an effective remedy for acts violating the fundamental rights granted to him by the constitution or by the law.
- No one shall be subjected to arbitrary arrest, detention, or exile.
- Everyone is entitled in full equality to a fair and public hearing by an ind
court, in the determination of his rights and obligations and of any criminal charge against him.
- Everyone has the right to freedom of movement and residence within the borders of each state. Everyone has the right to leave any country, including his own, and to return to his country.
- Everyone has the right to a nationality. No one shall be arbitrarily deprived of his nationality, nor denied the right to change his nationality.

In India, the National Human Rights Commission (NHRC) has been constituted under the Protection of Human Rights Act, 1993. This promotes and protects human rights in Indian society. In India, the celebration of Human Rights Day, on 10 December, gives us an opportunity to judge the status of human rights standards. The day is also celebrated to promote the universal human rights: to live and to do so peacefully. Human Rights issues in India relate to trafficking of women and children, food security, right to education and health, disappearance of people, displacement of people due to disasters, conflicts and development, child labour, deaths in police custody, and violation of human rights of prisoners and the disabled. On these issues, the Commission not only deals with individual cases but also issues guidelines for the implementing agencies.

COMPREHENSION

A. Choose the correct option.

1. Human Rights Day is celebrated on ....(*29 December/21 March/ 10 December*) every year.
2. The Universal Declaration of Human Rights says no one shall be subjected to ....(*sudden/legal/arbitrary*) arrest, detention, or exile.
3. The United Nations General Assembly proclaims the Universal Declaration of Human Rights as a common standard of achievement for people of .... (*Russia/India/all nations*).
4. In India, the National Human Rights Commission (NHRC) has been constituted under the Protection of Human Rights Act, ...(*1947/1852/1993*).
5. (*Human trafficking/Child labour/Political corruption*) ....is not a human rights issue.

B. Answer the questions in brief.

1. When did Human Rights Day come into being?

    ...

    ...

2. Mention any three rights included in the Universal Declaration of Human Rights.

    ...

    ...

3. What are the main human rights issues in India?

    ...

    ...

    ...

    ...

4. Find words in the passage which mean the following:

    a. famous and respected: ...

    b. not based on logic and seemingly unfair: ...

C. Think and answer the questions.

1. Is the right to nationality important? Give reasons for your answer.

    ...

    ...

    ...

    ...

    ...

    ...

2. Child labour is a serious problem in India. How can this problem be solved?

    ...

    ...

    ...

    ...

    ...

    ...

    ...

    ...

    ...

VOCABULARY

A. Fill in each blank with the correct word from the box.

maintain understand respectful acquaintance value friendship loyal misunderstanding

Building a lasting .... is not easy. An .... or a chance friendship may or may not turn into a lasting friendship. Many of us look for a good friend, but very few of us understand what it takes to .... a friendship. The first thing you should do is understand your friend as well as help your friend .... you. In case you notice any .... brewing, address that directly. You can enrich your friendship by making it interesting and adding .... to it. Right from the beginning of your friendship, always be at your friend's side and be .... to your friend. You and your friends may not have the same likes and dislikes. You should be .... of these differences.

Abbreviations and Acronyms

- An **abbreviation** is a shortened form of a word or a phrase. For example:

  NHRC (National Human Rights Commission)
  IAS (Indian Administrative Service)

- An **acronym** is usually formed with the initials of the words in a phrase or the name of something. The initials form and are pronounced as a word. For example:

  PAN (Permanent Account Number)
  RAW (Research and Analysis Wing)

B. Classify the following as abbreviations and acronyms and write their full form.

1. Capt. ....
2. dept ....
3. scuba ....
4. NATO ....
5. mph ....
6. St ....
7. a.m. ....
8. IMF ....
9. CEO ....
10. ISRO ....

DICTIONARY SKILLS

Look at the words in bold and say which part of speech each is. You may use dictionary if you like.

1. **Wow**, this is great news! ....
2. They went **into** the hall. ....
3. This is a **pretty** vase. ....
4. I want the **blue** ball. ....
5. **New York** is a big city. ....
6. We finished it **yesterday**. ....
7. Let's do **it**. ....
8. Remember to drive **safely**. ....
9. Should I wait for **you**? ....
10. Do you want to go out **or** stay at home? ....

GRAMMAR

Non-finite Verbs

- A **non-finite verb** is a form of a verb that does not show a distinction in number, person, or tense, and cannot stand alone as the main verb in a sentence.
- Non-finite verbs are of three kinds—infinitive, gerund and participle.

Infinitive

The infinitive is the base form of a verb. It is often used with *to* but sometimes without *to* as well. For example:

I like to read horror stories.
We saw him enter the house.

Gerund

The *-ing* form of a verb which is used as a noun is called a gerund. For example:

Cycling is good for health.

Participle

There are two main kinds of participles: present and past participles. They both act as adjectives.

- The **present participle** is formed by adding *-ing* to the base form of a verb. For example:

  The students are in the reading room.

- The **past participle** is formed by adding *-ed, -d, -t, -en, -n* to the base form of a verb. For example:

  Are these published poems?
  What did you do with the broken bat?

A. Underline non-finite verbs in the sentences and say what kind it is.

1. These freshly cooked beans are tasty..........................
2. The sleeping watchman was unaware of the burglary..........................
3. My cousin wants to learn French..........................
4. The doctor advised me to go for a walk daily..........................
5. My aunt sent me a handwritten letter last month..........................
6. She put the ironed clothes in the wardrobe..........................
7. Sailing is my favourite sport..........................
8. The teacher returned the checked notebooks to the students..........................
9. I am fond of writing horror stories..........................
10. We wanted to bring you a present..........................

B. Use non-finite forms of the verbs in sentences of your own: four infinitives, three gerunds, and three participles.

play	*sing*	*walk*	*sleep*	*dance*	*burn*	*eat*	*write*	*complete*	*learn*

1. ....
2. ....
3. ....
4. ....
5. ....
6. ....
7. ....
8. ....
9. ....
10. ....

Prepositions

A **preposition** is a word that comes before a noun or pronoun and shows the relationship between two words in a sentence. For example:

The girl is sitting on a chair.

In this example, the preposition *on* shows the relationship between the girl and the chair.

C. Fill in each blank with the correct preposition.

1. Raman is sitting .... a sofa.
2. I have met him only once .... the last month.
3. She has spent all her life .... Hyderabad.
4. The woman is putting something .... the oven.
5. The kitchen is .... the first floor.
6. I study science .... the morning.
7. The sports equipment is .... the basement.
8. I looked .... my nephew while his parents were out.
9. We should not stare .... people.
10. Farmers look forward .... a better standard of living.
11. The principal promised to look .... the matter.
12. I am looking .... my car keys.
13. We arrived .... New York at 3.30 in the morning.
14. You told him the truth .... time.
15. 'Old-fashioned' means .... fashion.

LISTENING AND SPEAKING

Listening

A. Listen carefully and fill in the blanks.

1. A lot of women gave birth to babies with severe ....deformities during the late 1950s.
2. The cause was the .... use of thalidomide.
3. The victims then decided to fight against the .... manufacturer.
4. *The* .... *Times* decided to publish a detailed article about it.
5. The European Court of Human Rights supported *The Sunday Times*'s right to .... of expression.

Speaking

B. Deliver an extempore speech on an ideal world with justice and equality.

WRITING

A. The Syrian war is one of the greatest examples of the violation of human rights in recent history. Write a paragraph expressing your opinion on the subject.

....

....

....

....

....

....

....

....

....

....

B. You have been selected as a debater for your school in a state-level competition. You are asked to send your biographical note within 100 words. Look at this example of a personal biographical note and then write your biographical note.

Ranjan Mazumdar is a student of class VIII of S. D. Memorial School, Ranchi. He is reputed to be a champion debater for his school. When he isn't studying, he spends time working on his computer, reading science fiction, and drawing pictures of people in the street. He is currently working on a project with the students of St Mary's School, Cochin, Kerala.

While writing your biographical note, keep these points in mind.

- Write in the third person.
- Start with your name.
- Say where you study.
- Describe your achievements.
- Talk about your goals and hobbies.

....

....

....

....

3 Partition

VOCABULARY

Rhyme Scheme

The **rhyme scheme** is the pattern in which the lines of a poem rhyme. The end rhyme of the first line is called *a*. If the next line rhymes with the first line, we call it *a* as well. A new line that doesn't rhyme with the first line is called *b*. We continue through the poem writing new letters for new ending sounds and matching letters for matching sounds. For example, look at these stanzas from R. L. Stevenson's poem *The Cow*.

The friendly cow all red and white, a
I love with all my heart: b
She gives me cream with all her might, a
To eat with apple tart. b

She wanders lowing here and there, c
And yet she cannot stray, d
All in the pleasant open air, c
The pleasant light of day; d

The rhyme scheme of the first stanza is *abab* and the second stanza is *cdcd*.

A. Write the rhyme scheme of each stanza of this poem.

Reeds of Innocence

Piping down the valleys wild,
Piping songs of pleasant glee,
On a cloud I saw a child,
And he laughing said to me:

'Pipe a song about a lamb!'
So I piped with merry cheer.
'Piper, pipe that song again;'
So I piped: he wept to hear.

'Drop thy pipe, thy happy pipe;
Sing thy songs of happy cheer!'
So I sung the same again,
While he wept with joy to hear.

'Piper, sit thee down and write
In a book that all may read.'
So he vanish'd from my sight;
And I pluck'd a hollow reed,

And I made a rural pen,
And I stain'd the water clear,
And I wrote my happy songs
Every child may joy to hear.

–William Blake

....

....

....

Homophones

Homophones are words that have the same pronunciation but different spellings and meanings. For example:

male – mail *week – weak*

B. Fill in each blank with the correct word.

flour	*flower*	*great*	*grate*	*here*	*hear*	*hole*	*whole*	*knew*	*new*

1. This curtain has a ....
2. She ate the .... pizza alone.
3. I can't .... you well; please speak a little louder.
4. Mukul, your notebook is lying ....
5. I had to .... carrots to make the dish.
6. My sister wants to be a .... footballer.
7. .... is the main ingredient in bread.

8. The rose is a beautiful ....

9. I .... the answer to the fourth question.

10. She bought a .... pair of shoes yesterday.

WRITING

Poster

- A **poster** is a large notice, message or advertisement put on display to create social awareness about something or to advertise something.
- Posters usually include both text and illustrations, though it is not mandatory.
- A poster should be appealing and it should give a powerful message.
- It should include all necessary details like the date, time and venue of the event advertised as well as the name of the issuing authority.
- The message should be delivered through catchy slogans and short sentences. Look at this sample poster.

Meet Your Best friends: Books

Read something every day,
Don't delay.

Read more,
Have more ideas.

Books inform,
instruct & entertain.

Thousands of books are waiting in the school library to give you new ideas.

Reading hours: 10 a.m. to 1 p.m.

Issued by XYZ School

Your school is organising a drive to help the poor by giving them warm clothes for winter. Make a poster appealing to people to donate clothes for the poor. Include all necessary details with the message. Also, draw appealing pictures to illustrate your message.

TEST 1

(20 marks)

VOCABULARY ....(5)

Fill in the blanks with a word from the list below.

right	*innocent*	*participate*	*violate*	*property*

1. The most well-known intellectual ....types are copyrights, patents, trademarks and trade secrets.
2. Indian citizens enjoy ....to freedom of expression.
3. Right to ....in the electoral process is one of the most important political rights in many countries.
4. Individuals may try to ....right of the freedom of thought and expression but the leadership or government has the duty to protect it.
5. One should be treated as ....until proven guilty in the court of law.

GRAMMAR..(10)

A. Change the sentences as directed. (5)

1. The Judge asked the Police to file a case against the persons accused in the violation of freedom of movement of the petitioner. (Interrogative sentence)
2. Did she protest against eve-teasing? (Negative sentence)
3. You must not go out without wearing face mask. (Imperative sentence)
4. How beautiful she is! (Declarative sentence)
5. It was an excellent photographic exhibition. (Exclamatory sentence)

B. Fill in the blanks with the appropriate preposition (5)

1. A violation of human rights occurs when a Government fails ....its obligations to ensure them.
2. Sometimes violation of one of the human rights is linked ....a violation of other rights.
3. Do you think that forcibly evicting people ....their homes is a violation of their right?

4. Is failure to pay a minimum wage .... a worker a violation of rights at work?
5. Isn't it a duty of the Government to prevent starvation .... all areas and communities in the State?

WRITING ....(5)

Write a description of how you feel about your online class during the Covid19 pandemic. You may write about what you like about it and what you don't like so much.

....

....

....

....

....

....

....

....

....

....

....

....

....

....

....

....

....

....

....

....

....

....

....

....

....

4 The Landlady

READING

Read this story about a man's hallucinations.

Staley Fleming's Hallucination

Of the two men who were talking, one was a physician.

'I sent for you, Doctor,' said the other, 'but I don't think you can do me any good. Maybe you can recommend a specialist in psychopathy. I fancy I'm a bit loony.'

'You look all right,' the physician said.

'I have hallucinations. I wake every night and see a big black Newfoundland dog in my room.'

'You say you wake; are you sure about that? "Hallucinations" are sometimes only dreams.'

'Oh, I wake all right. Sometimes I lie still a long time, looking at the dog as earnestly as the dog looks at me. When I can't endure it any longer, I sit up in bed—and nothing is there!'

'What is the beast's expression?'

'It seems to me sinister. This is not a real animal. Newfoundland dogs are pretty mild-looking, you know; what's the matter with this one?'

'Really, my diagnosis would have no value: I am not going to treat the dog.'

The physician laughed at his own pleasantry. He then said: 'Fleming, your description of the beast fits the dog of the late Atwell Barton.'

Fleming half rose from his chair, and sat again. 'I remember Barton,' he said; 'I believe he was—it was reported that—wasn't there something suspicious about his death?'

The physician said: 'Three years ago, the body of your old enemy,

Atwell Barton, was found in the woods near his house and yours. He had been stabbed to death. There have been no arrests; there was no clue. Some of us had *theories*. I had one. Have you?'

'I? What could I know about it? You remember that I left for Europe almost immediately afterwards. In the few weeks since my return, I have not given the matter a thought. What about his dog?'

'It was the first to find the body. It died of starvation on his grave.'

The night wind brought in through the open window the long wailing howl of a distant dog. Staley Fleming strode several times across the room in the steadfast gaze of the physician; then, abruptly confronting him, almost shouted: 'What has all this to do with my trouble, Dr Halderman? You forget why you were sent for.'

Rising, the physician laid his hand upon his patient's arm and said, gently: 'Pardon me. I cannot diagnose your disorder offhand—tomorrow, perhaps. Please go to bed, leaving your door unlocked; I will pass the night here with your books. Can you call me without rising?'

'Yes, there is an electric bell.'

'Good. If anything disturbs you, push the button without sitting up. Good night.'

Sitting comfortably in an armchair, the man of medicine stared into the glowing coals and thought deep and long. Soon he fell asleep, and when he woke, it was past midnight. He lifted a book from the table at his side and looked at the title. It was Denneker's *Meditations*. He opened it at random and began to read: 'For as much as it is ordained of God that all flesh hath spirit and thereby taketh on spiritual powers, so, also, the spirit hath powers of the flesh, even when it is gone out of the flesh and liveth as a thing apart, as many a violence performed by wraith and lemure sheweth.—'

The reading was interrupted by a shaking of the house, as by the fall of a heavy object. The reader flung down the book, rushed from the room and mounted the stairs to Fleming's bed chamber. He tried the door, but contrary to his instructions, it was locked. He broke it open. On the floor, near the disordered bed, lay Fleming, gasping away his life.

The physician raised the dying man's head from the floor and observed a wound in his throat. 'I should have thought of this,' he said, believing it suicide.

When the man was dead, an examination disclosed the unmistakable marks of an animal's fangs deeply sunken into the jugular vein. But there was no animal.

– Ambrose Bierce

COMPREHENSION

A. Mark the statements as true (T) or false (F).

1. Staley Fleming was talking to a specialist in psychopathy. ☐
2. Fleming said he had hallucinations every afternoon. ☐
3. The doctor said sometimes hallucinations are just dreams. ☐
4. The doctor said Fleming's description of the dog matched the late Atwell Barton's dog. ☐
5. The doctor advised Fleming to go to bed leaving his door open. ☐

B. Answer the questions in brief.

1. What hallucinations did Staley Fleming have?

....

....

2. Who was Atwell Barton? How did he die?

....

....

3. What happened to Barton's dog after his death?

....

....

4. What did the physician advise Fleming to do?

....

....

5. What was the title of the book the doctor picked up to read?

....

....

6. Write the meaning of each word in the context of the passage.
   a. psychopathy: ....
   b. loony: ....
   c. sinister: ....
   d. pleasantry: ....

C. Think and answer the questions.

1. Describe the examination report. Was it shocking? If yes, why?

....

....

....

2. Do you think Fleming committed suicide? Justify your answer.

....

....

....

VOCABULARY

Phrasal Verbs

- A **phrasal verb** is a phrase consisting of a main verb and a preposition or an adverb, or both.
- Phrasal verbs can be transitive when they have an object or intransitive when they do not take any object. For example:

  ring up – to call   *take off* – to remove
- It is better to restrict the use of phrasal verbs in a formal conversation or writing.

A. Fill in each blank with the correct phrasal verb.

1. Friends can help you to .... (*get around/get by/get through*) a difficult time in life.
2. I'm tired because I .... (*got around/got on/got up*) at 5 in the morning.
3. What information about the scientist are you .... (*looking for/looking at/looking about*)?
4. I have given Samanth Prabhu the task of .... (*sorting out/sorting through/sorting with*) the students' projects.
5. I .... (*found for/found in/found out*) about your exam result from your brother.
6. He skipped the match because he thought he didn't .... (*fit for/fit in/fit with*) the team.
7. The match was .... (*called off/called for/called by*) because of rain.
8. I think he will .... (*get out/get in/get through*) the entrance exam.
9. The teacher encouraged the students to .... (*keep back/keep up/keep down*) the good work.
10. Smriti had forgotten to .... (*put on/put up with/put across*) her new wristwatch.

Collocations

In English, some words are often used together as they sound natural together. This is known as **collocation**. For example:

heavy rain   *scenic view*   *sweet smell*   *maintain discipline*

B. Fill in each blank with the correct word from the box.

conclusion	*utter*	*classical*	*hatch*	*heinous*	*committed*	*major*	*keep*	*farewell*	*historical*

1. I love .... music.
2. Pollution is a .... problem the world faces today.
3. I'm afraid the result of the match was a foregone ....
4. The room was in .... chaos; things were lying all over the floor.
5. The police say he is involved in .... crimes.
6. He says he has never .... any crime.
7. We should always .... the promises we make.
8. How many days do the eggs take to ....?
9. We visited some .... monuments in China.
10. The students bade .... to the outgoing principal.

GRAMMAR

Tenses

Let us recapitulate **tenses**.

Tense	Present	Past	Future
Simple	I *play* chess every day.	I *played chess* yesterday.	I *will play* chess tomorrow.
Continuous	I *am playing* chess now.	I *was playing* chess at that time.	I *will be playing* chess tomorrow.
Perfect	I *have played* five games of chess so far.	I *had played* five games of chess before you joined me.	When my mother comes back, I *will have* already *played* at least ten games of chess.
Perfect continuous	I *have been playing* chess for two hours now.	When my mother came, I *had been playing* chess for three hours.	When my mother comes back, I *will have been playing* chess for several hours.

A. Fill in each blank with the correct tense of the verb.

1. My father .... (*go*) for a walk every morning. It helps him stay healthy.
2. I .... (*write*) three stories and I'm tired now. I will write the remaining stories later.
3. By the time my father returns this evening, I .... (*clean*) the whole house.
4. She .... (*work*) on this project for the last three weeks.
5. My brother .... (*miss*) his exams because he was ill.
6. I'm busy now. I .... (*talk*) to you later about that matter.
7. My sister .... (*go*) to sleep before I returned home.
8. I .... (*give*) your message to him when I meet him this evening.

B. Change the tense of each sentence as indicated.

1. I play tennis with my sister. (*present continuous*)

   ....

2. I have been living in Dehradun for five years. (*present perfect*)

   ....

3. I will visit my grandparents tomorrow. (*future continuous*)

   ....

4. He jogged every morning. (*simple present*)

   ....

5. She had completed two chapters. (*future perfect*)

   ....

6. We have been playing hockey for three hours. (*past perfect*)

   ....

7. Lina draws ten pictures every day. (*simple future*)

   ....

8. Navit likes the pictures Lina draws. (*simple past*)

   ....

9. The teacher is writing the exercise on the board. (*past continuous*)

   ....

10. Simran and Aman do their work with great diligence. (*simple past*)

    ....

Question Tags

- **Question tags** are short questions added to the end of statements. They usually seek confirmation of what the statement says or to emphasise the idea. For example:

  I didn't say you are right, did I?

  Your father is a doctor, isn't he?

- If the statement is positive, we add a negative question tag to it.

  You have a good dictionary, don't you?

  She lives in Delhi, doesn't she?

- If the statement is negative, we use a positive question tag to it.

  This is not a good watch, is it?

  They won't come today, will they?

C. Add appropriate question tags to the statements.

1. He is an honest person, ...?
2. I have always helped you overcome difficulties, ...?
3. Delhi is too crowded, ...?
4. There is no harm in walking, ...?
5. These biscuits don't taste good, ...?
6. You didn't send me any message, ...?
7. You can't lift this box alone, ...?
8. We should respect everybody's opinion, ...?
9. Anita completes her work on time, ...?
10. I have already shared this information with you, ...?
11. The children did not watch TV, ...?
12. Sarita's father is not an engineer, ...?
13. They are going for a picnic this weekend, ...?
14. We are going to see the film today, ...?
15. He is collecting stamps for his school project, ...?

LISTENING AND SPEAKING

Listening

Listen to a passage carefully and answer the questions.

1. What is ergonomics?

   ....

   ....

2. What does an ergonomist take into account while redesigning a machine?

3. What is the traditional approach of selecting a person to operate a machine?

4. What is the new approach adopted in ergonomics?

5. What are the main subjects an ergonomist needs to have a good knowledge of?

WRITING

Brochure

- A **brochure** is one of the most popular communication tools to give people information about something or to advertise something.
- It usually gives information in an appealing way and it can have pictures, too.

The Himalayan Club is going to organise its annual Mountain Film Fest in association with the Cultural Centre in Kolkata on 3 May 2018. Make a brochure for the event.

Keep these points in mind while making your brochure.

- Aim at making the brochure appealing to your target audience.
- Think about the purpose of the brochure, for example, to persuade, to entertain, or to inform.
- The text should be concise and accurate.
- Use short and simple sentences.
- Choose graphics carefully. Try to achieve a balanced presentation.
- At the end of the brochure, include a call to action.
- Include contact information at the end.
- Proofread and edit your brochure to ensure there are no errors.

5 While the Auto Waits

READING

Read this poem about haunted houses.

Haunted Houses

All houses wherein men have lived and died
Are haunted houses. Through the open doors
The harmless phantoms on their errands glide,
With feet that make no sound upon the floors.

We meet them at the doorway, on the stair,
Along the passages they come and go,
Impalpable impressions on the air,
A sense of something moving to and fro.

There are more guests at table than the hosts
Invited; the illuminated hall
Is thronged with quiet, inoffensive ghosts,
As silent as the pictures on the wall.

The stranger at my fireside cannot see
The forms I see, nor hear the sounds I hear;
He but perceives what is; while unto me
All that has been is visible and clear.

– H.W. Longfellow

COMPREHENSION

A. Read the lines from the poem and answer the questions.

1. *All houses wherein men have lived and died*
   Are haunted houses. Through the open doors
   The harmless phantoms on their errands glide,
   With feet that make no sound upon the floors.

   a. What houses does the poet say are haunted?

   ....

   b. What kind of feet do the harmless phantoms have, according to the poet?

   ....

2. *We meet them at the doorway, on the stair,*
   Along the passages they come and go,
   Impalpable impressions on the air,
   A sense of something moving to and fro.

   a. Who does 'they' here refer to?

   ....

   b. What kind of impressions do 'they' create?

   ....

B. Answer the questions in brief.

1. Where do we meet the harmless phantoms?

   ....

   ....

2. What happens at the table?

   ....

   ....

3. What is the illuminated hall thronged with?

   ....

   ....

4. How do the speaker and the stranger by his fireside perceive things differently?

   ....

   ....

5. Find words in the poem that mean the following:

   a. that is easily noticed by the mind or the senses: ....

   b. lit with bright lights: ....

C. Think and answer the questions.

1. Give an example of a simile from the poem and explain the comparison made.

2. Give an example of alliteration from the poem and explain what creates the alliteration in it.

3. What impression of the phantoms do you get from the poem?

VOCABULARY

Say whether these words use British English spelling or American English spelling. Then write the other spelling of each.

1. fibre
2. fueled
3. pediatric
4. offense
5. traveller
6. endeavour
7. caliber
8. monolog
9. fulfill
10. chequered
11. humor
12. licence
13. centimeter
14. grey
15. center

Phrases

- A **phrase** is a group of words. It does not have a subject or a finite verb.
- It cannot express a complete idea on its own. For example:

in the park *out of three* *outside the room*

Let us study the four main kinds of phrases:

Noun phrase

A **noun phrase** acts as a noun. For example:

I have a beautiful dress.

The naughty boy broke the plates.

Prepositional phrase

A **prepositional phrase** has a preposition and its object (noun or pronoun). For example:

The children were playing outside the house.

He put the apples in the basket.

Adjective phrase

An **adjective phrase** acts like an adjective. It modifies a noun or a pronoun. For example:

He has a phone with a big screen.

He wears a chain of gold.

Adverb phrase

An **adverb phrase** acts like an adverb. It modifies an adjective or a verb in a sentence. For example:

Lina spoke in a low voice.

I entered the house after him.

Underline the phrases in the sentences and state their kind.

1. He wore a turban of cotton. ....
2. There I met a girl with golden hair. ....
3. He was a man of great wealth. ....
4. He is sleeping on the floor. ....
5. The girl sat beside her mother. ....
6. He stayed there for a few hours. ....

7. Divya is sitting in the car. ....

8. He has a dog with a short tail. ....

9. The teacher explained the poem in simple language. ....

10. He bought a nice white shirt yesterday. ....

11. Everybody laughed at the cartoon. ....

12. Lina won the contest against all odds. ....

13. There was a bucket full of water. ....

14. He was walking very slowly. ....

Speaking

Work in groups of four and enact the play *While the Auto Waits* or a play of your choice. You can also add to the play script. For example, the person playing the man/girl in the park can say more things to show that he/she comes from a poor/royal family. Take care of the intonation while delivering your dialogues.

WRITING

Write a report for your school magazine on the topic *Parents' Attitude Towards Higher Education for Girls in Rural India.* A magazine report includes these features.

- Headline/Title
- Byline (your name and class)
- Body of the report (all necessary details)

TEST 2 (20 marks)

VOCABULARY ....(5)

Match the two parts of the collocations

1.	normal	a.	house
2.	indian	b.	film
3.	horror	c.	diet
4.	haunted	d.	procedures
5.	established	e.	citizen

GRAMMAR ....(10)

A. Complete the text with the simple past or past perfect form of the verbs in brackets. (5)

Something strange happened to me last night. It was 8 o'clock, and I'd .... (have) a long and tedious day. I was tired and lonely, so I .... (decide) to stop by the marine drive. I sat on some steps and closed my eyes. After a few minutes, I fell asleep.

When I .... (wake) up, I found the moon had .... (move) behind a cloud. Suddenly, I heard a splash. I looked down at the water and saw something strange lurking in the water. Initially, I was so .... (terrify) that I closed my eyes. But I opened them, I could see a green monster in the water.

B. Match statements 1 to 5 with to question tags a to e. (5)

1.	I saw a strange monster in the sea.	a.	can I?
2.	I can't open my eyes.	b.	don't you?
3.	You love animals.	c.	didn't I?
4.	There are more than six applicants for the post.	d.	haven't they?
5.	A few families have hundreds of cable channels at home.	e.	aren't there?

WRITING .... (5)

Write a review of your school magazine which has been just published. In your review you should include

- how you feel while reading the magazine
- whether the content, topics focus on news or entertainment
- what in the magazine makes you want to read more
- how you feel about the positives and negatives of the magazine and your overall opinion or rating.

6 Journey to Jo'burg

READING

Read this passage about Ahmed Kathrada's struggle against apartheid in South Africa.

Ahmed Kathrada

Former South African President Nelson Mandela with Kathrada in Johannesburg

Ahmed Kathrada, South Africa's revered Indian-origin anti-apartheid activist and one of Nelson Mandela's closest aides, played a major role in shaping the country's post-apartheid policies. Affectionately known as Uncle Kathy, Kathrada was born on 21 August 1929, to immigrant Indian parents in the small town of Schweizer-Reneke in Western Transvaal (now North West Province). His parents, Mohamed and Hawa Kathrada, were Bohra Muslims who hailed from Surat in Gujarat.

The town of Schweizer-Reneke didn't have any schools for Indian-origin children, who were not allowed to attend local primary schools. So at an early age, Kathrada moved to Johannesburg, which had a school for Indians, to live with his aunt Fatima.

During his childhood, Kathrada was deeply influenced by the Transvaal Indian Congress (TIC), initially called the Transvaal British Indian Association (TBIA) and founded in 1903 by Mahatma Gandhi to fight discrimination against Indians in South Africa.

At the young age of twelve, Kathrada began distributing leaflets at street corners for the Young Communist League of South Africa. After finishing school at the age of seventeen, Kathrada began working full-time in the offices of the Transvaal Passive Resistance Council and played an important role in the protests against the Asiatic Land Tenure and Indian Representation Act. This discriminatory act sought to define the areas where Indians could live, trade, and own land while giving them limited political representation.

Kathrada served his first jail sentence for civil disobedience when he was imprisoned along with 2,000 other volunteers while protesting against the law. He later became general secretary of the Transvaal Indian Congress and was instrumental in linking it to the African National Congress (ANC). This was the time he met and became close friends with ANC leaders like Nelson Mandela, Walter Sisulu, Ismail Meer, and J. N. Singh.

A founding member of the Transvaal Indian Volunteer Corps, Kathrada enrolled at Witwatersrand University in 1951. The same year, he visited the concentration camps of Auschwitz, an experience that affected him deeply and left him convinced that racism needed to be eradicated in South Africa.

Abandoning his studies, Kathrada devoted himself fully to political activism. He helped organise the Campaign of Defiance against Unjust Laws.

Kathrada was one of the famous Rivonia 11—including Nelson Mandela, Dennis Goldberg, Walter Sisulu, Govan Mbeki, Elias Motsoaledi, Raymond Mhlaba and Andrew Mlangeni—who were arrested in 1962 while having a secret meeting at Liliesleaf Farm in Rivonia. Eight of the accused, including Kathrada, were sentenced to life imprisonment with hard labour on Robben Island. In an interview to the *Mail Guardian*, Kathrada said: 'The moment that stood out for me at the Rivonia Trial would be the end of Mandela's speech where he said, "I have fought against white domination, and I have fought against black domination. I have cherished the ideal of a democratic and free society in which all persons live together in harmony with equal opportunities. It is an ideal which I hope to live for and achieve. But if need be, it is an ideal for which I am prepared to die."'

He spent the next twenty-six years and three months in prison, including eighteen years in apartheid's most notorious prison, Robben Island. Kathrada used his time in prison to obtain four university degrees: a BA, a B. Bibliography, and two BA Honours degrees.

Kathrada was sixty when he was at last freed, in October 1989, just months before Mandela himself walked free. In 1994, when Mandela was elected the first entirely democratic president of South Africa, he appointed Kathrada his parliamentary counsellor in the first all-race ANC government.

Later, Kathrada started Ahmed Kathrada Foundation to work against racism and chaired the Robben Island museum, preserving the prison as part of South Africa's heritage. He also wrote several memorable books, including *No Bread for Mandela: Memoirs of Ahmed Kathrada*.

In 2005, Kathrada was honoured with the *Pravasi Bharatiya Samman Award*, India's highest honour for foreign nationals of Indian origin.

In 2017, he died at a hospital in Johannesburg after struggling with a brief illness following brain surgery.

COMPREHENSION

A. Mark the statements as true (T) or false (F).

1. Kathrada moved to Johannesburg to live with his aunt Fatima and study there. ☐
2. Kathrada served his first jail sentence for civil disobedience. ☐
3. Kathrada was released from prison in 1989. ☐
4. Kathrada was honoured with the Bharat Ratna in 2004. ☐
5. He wrote the book *No Bread for Mandela: Memoirs of Ahmed Kathrada*. ☐
6. Kathrada died at a hospital in Delhi in 2016. ☐

B. Answer the questions in brief.

1. When and where was Kathrada born? Where were his parents originally from?

   ....

   ....

2. Why did Kathrada move to Johannesberg in childhood?

   ....

   ....

3. Who was the founder of TBIA? When and why was TBIA formed?

   ....

   ....

4. Who does 'the famous Rivonia 11' refer to? What happened to them?

   ....

   ....

5. Why was Kathrada sentenced to life imprisonment?

   ....

   ....

6. How did he spend his time in prison?

   ....

   ....

7. What is the *Pravasi Bharatiya Samman Award?* When did Kathrada win it?

   ....

   ....

8. Find the antonym of the following word in the passage.

   emigrants ....

C. Think and answer the questions.

1. What influenced Kathrada to join South Africa's struggle against apartheid?

....

....

....

2. *Kathrada was a man of courage and determination.* Justify the statement.

....

....

....

VOCABULARY

A. Write the meaning of each word.

1. discriminatory: ....
2. affected: ....
3. documented: ....
4. imprisonment: ....
5. domination: ....
6. harmony: ....
7. notorious: ....
8. initially: ....
9. accused: ....
10. honoured: ....

B. Write two antonyms of each word.

1. discriminatory ....
2. entirely ....
3. documented ....
4. imprisonment ....
5. major ....
6. harmony ....
7. notorious ....
8. initially ....
9. accused ....
10. honoured ....

Clauses

- A **clause** is a group of words that has a subject and a predicate containing a finite verb. It can stand alone as a sentence or be a part of a sentence.
- There are three kinds of clauses:

Noun clause

- It acts like a noun and can be the subject, object or complement of a verb. For example:

  I didn't say that he was a poet.

  Tell me who broke the window.

Adjective clause or relative clause

- It modifies or defines a noun or pronoun. For example:

  There was a dog that had long ears.

  The boy who is bowling is my brother.

Adverb clause

- It tells us about the action of the verb in the main clause. It tells us the time, place, reason, manner, condition, or result of the action. For example:

  He visited my house after I had left for school.

  She behaved as if she were a celebrity.

A. Underline the noun clauses (NC), adjective clauses (AC) and adverb clauses (AVC) in the sentences. Then mention what kind each clause is.

1. I have a storybook that has beautiful illustrations. [ ]
2. She became so emotional that she could not speak. [ ]
3. Do you know what he wrote in the mail? [ ]
4. The duck went where it could swim without any fear. [ ]
5. I do not sing because I tend to go off-key. [ ]
6. Uncle Prateek met them when he was in Mexico. [ ]
7. The book was lying where I had left it. [ ]
8. I cannot understand why you don't want to exercise. [ ]
9. I know an artist who can draw pictures very fast. [ ]
10. She visits her cousins whenever she goes to Mumbai. [ ]

B. Complete the sentences with appropriate clauses and say what kind they are.

1. Sonakshi told me ....
2. This is the book ....

3. I saw a strange animal ....
4. The principal rewarded the girl ....
5. I don't think ....
6. The coach gave one more chance to the players ....

Punctuation

Hyphen

A **hyphen** (-) is a small symbol used as a punctuation mark. It has three main uses.

- Hyphens are used in many compound words. For example:

  value-added *computer-generated*

- They are used to join some prefixes to words, especially if the prefix ends in a vowel and the word begins with a vowel. For example:

  re-examine

- They are also used to divide words at the end of a line if there is not enough space for the whole word. For example:

  After a long struggle and sacrifices of lots of brave, patriotic people, India finally got indepen-dence in 1947.

Dash

A **dash** (—) is a punctuation mark used when we want to add something to what we have just said. For example:

I didn't mean your answer is wrong—I meant both the answers are right.

Ellipsis

An **ellipsis** (...) is a set of three dots. It is used to indicate that a word, words or sentences have been left out. For example:

I wanted to help him... there is no use talking about the past now.

C. Punctuate the sentences correctly by inserting hyphens, dashes and ellipses wherever necessary.

1. Paulo Coelho is a world famous writer.
2. This a computer generated password.
3. I didn't say your performance is poor I meant you can do even better.
4. It was a neck to neck fight and nobody could say who'd win ultimately it was sportsmanship that won.
5. I like this book a lot it's one of the most interesting spy novels ever.
6. Do you know the grey haired woman?
7. This is the second highest award given in sports.
8. I don't know when I fell asleep it was eight in the morning and I was late for school.

LISTENING AND SPEAKING

Listening

Listen carefully and choose the correct option.

1. According to the writer, the best talents of our age are devoted to
   a. the study of sociology.
   b. the study of the outward or material world.
   c. the study of religion.
2. They study the beginning of the organic life and its progress
   a. from the lowest to the highest stages.
   b. from the poorest to the richest stages.
   c. from the youngest to the oldest stages.
3. Apart from the material world, there is
   a. an inward intellectual world, too.
   b. an outward intellectual world, too.
   c. an inward physical world, too.
4. In the study of the history of the human mind, India occupies a place
   a. second to only the USA.
   b. second to only China.
   c. second to none, that is, the first in the world.

WRITING

Argumentative Essay

- An **argumentative essay** expresses the writer's point of view about a subject. While supporting or opposing a particular point of view, it also includes the opposite view, though only to refute.
- The objective of the essay is to convince the readers that the writer's stand is right.

Write an argumentative essay on the topic: *All Students Should Have the Right to Choose their Subjects.*

Keep these points in mind while writing the essay.

- Introduce the subject. You can also use a quote or proverb to do that.
- Explain the issue or controversy clearly including both sides of the story.
- Take your stand, explaining why you believe in it.

- Convince the readers about your point of view.
- Think of any objections that can be raised and put forth your arguments cohesively.
- Conclude the essay with a strong statement, in support of your views.

7 A Ballad of Sir Pertab Singh

VOCABULARY

Simile

A **simile** is a figure of speech that makes a comparison between two dissimilar things, using the words *like* or *as*. For example:

He is as cunning as a fox.

The sea roared like a lion.

A. Circle the simile in each sentence. Also, explain each comparison.

1. Listening to the scientist's spellbinding speech, the students were as quiet as mice.
   are compared to ....
2. The young man looked as strong as a bull.
   is compared to ....
3. The English paper was as tricky as a labyrinth.
   is compared to ....
4. She hung her head like a dying flower.
   is compared to ....
5. The clouds were like ice cream castles in the sky.
   are compared to ....
6. The children ran like ripples through water.
   are compared to ....

7. Her hands fluttered like hummingbirds' wings.

.... are compared to ....

8. The river flows like a stream of glass.

.... is compared to ....

9. Her eyes are like those of statues.

.... are compared to ....

10. Bhavya is as busy as a bee.

.... is compared to ....

B. Use similes to describe how you feel on these occasions.

1. How do you feel on a Sunday morning?

....

2. How do you feel celebrating Republic Day at your school?

....

3. How do you feel on your birthday?

....

4. How did you feel on the first day of your school?

....

5. How do you feel when you win a competition?

....

C. Complete these compound words. The first letter of the second word that forms part of the word is also given.

1. grassh ....
2. passp ....
3. rattles ....
4. scapeg ....
5. pepperm ....
6. toothp ....
7. babys ....
8. honeyc ....
9. keyh ....
10. washr ....
11. wastew ....
12. waterp ....
13. raind ....
14. houseb ....
15. tables ....
16. teamm ....

Slogans

A **slogan** is a catchphrase or motto of a business company, a political party, or any other organisation or institution.

Here are a few steps you can follow to write a slogan.

- Collect information about the organisation or product that you are writing the slogan for.
- Try to identify what makes the organisation or the product different from its competitors.
- Find some popular slogans and think why they are so popular or catchy.
- Write down taglines that come to your mind.
- Narrow down to some of the best options.
- Keep writing and rewriting till you have something short and catchy that goes with the brand of the organisation or the product.

A. Write three slogans for your school with the aim of informing people about your school's motto and the quality of education it provides.

....

....

....

....

....

....

B. Match these slogans with the organisations or the products they represent. Then create a new slogan for each one.

Slogan	Product
1. Experience real-world video games	car
2. Explore the Himalayas	computer
3. Don't just drive but cruise	bread
4. Tastes best	travel company
5. Give wings to your feet	shoes

C. Write two slogans for each of these campaigns.

1. Clean India

2. Abolish Child Labour

3. Educate Girls

4. Save Water

....

....

5. Save Trees

....

....

8 Across the Sahara on a Bicycle

READING

Read this poem in which a mother is motivating her son.

Mother to Son

Well, son, I'll tell you:
Life for me ain't been no crystal stair.
It's had tacks in it,
And splinters,
And boards torn up,
And places with no carpet on the floor—
Bare.

But all the time
I'se been a-climbin' on,
And reachin' landin's,
And turnin' corners,
And sometimes goin' in the dark
Where there ain't been no light.

So boy, don't you turn back.
Don't you set down on the steps
'Cause you finds it's kinder hard.
Don't you fall now—
For I'se still goin', honey,
I'se still climbin',
And life for me ain't been no crystal stair.

– *Langston Hughes*

COMPREHENSION

A. Read the lines from the poem and answer the questions.

1. *Well, son, I'll tell you:*
   Life for me ain't been no crystal stair.
   a. Who is the speaker here?
   ....
   b. What does 'no crystal stair' mean here?
   ....
2. *For I'se still goin', honey,*
   I'se still climbin',
   And life for me ain't been no crystal stair.
   a. Who does 'honey' refer to here?
   ....
   b. What does 'I'se still climbin' mean?
   ....

B. Answer the questions in brief.

1. What is the mother telling her son in the first stanza?
   ....
   ....
2. What do 'tacks' and 'splinters' in the poem signify?
   ....
   ....
3. What does the woman say she's been doing all the time?
   ....
   ....
4. Find two metaphors in the poem.
   ....
   ....

C. Think and answer the questions.

1. Describe the mother's nature. What kind of person do you think she is?
   ....
   ....
   ....

2. The poem gives us a message about life. What is it?

VOCABULARY

Compound Words

- **Compound words** are words formed by joining two or more words. They are generally of three types:
    - Closed compound words

      They are written as one word without any hyphen or space. For example:

      keyboard *textbook* *desktop*
    - Open compound words

      They are written as two words with no hyphen. For example:

      post office *mobile phone* *living room*
    - Hyphenated compound words

      They are two or more words connected with a hyphen. For example:

      well-being *short-term* *up-to-date*
- We also hyphenate compound words to avoid any possible ambiguity. For example:

  re-pair (to pair again) *re-form* (to form again)
- Most compound words formed with prefixes have no hyphens. For example:

  extracurricular *multipurpose* *bilingual*
- Compounds words formed with some prefixes like *self-* are hyphenated. For example:

  self-care *self-esteem* *self-directed*

A. Correct mistakes in the sentences, if any. Put a tick (✓) against the sentences that are correct.

1. Tanima is a well respected actress.
2. Manisha bought an extra large T-shirt for her brother.
3. We arrived at the stadium at half time.
4. It is his part time job.
5. My brother is no longer a school student; he is in college now.
6. The nineteen year old archer has won a medal at the Asian Games.
7. The India Pakistan cricket series was very exciting.
8. Self study is necessary for the reinforcement of concepts learnt at school.

B. Unscramble the jumbled words and fill in the blanks with the words formed.

1. Raman's father cooks .... (*EOSDIUICL*) pasta.
2. The teacher was .... (*MESSIREPD*) with Vibhor's marks.
3. A good book is one's best .... (*ONPANMCIO*).
4. Dev likes to .... (*SENTLI*) to rock music.
5. Plants need .... (*LUHIGTSN*) to make their own food.
6. We must .... (*EOYB*) our parents and teachers.
7. .... (*RAILP*) is the fourth month of the year.
8. The cat .... (*SCHEAD*) the mice in the barn.
9. The weather is .... (*AASNPLET*) today.
10. The moon .... (*OSHNE*) brightly over the mountains.
11. Shakespeare is my favourite .... (*THOARU*).

C. Fill in each blank with the correct phrasal verb. Make sure to use the correct tense.

hurry up	*give up*	*come off*	*think of*	*come across*
	take off	*bring up*	*put on*	

1. What do you .... the new plan?
2. I have .... the bad habit of waking up late.
3. Don't forget to .... a life jacket before going boating in the lake.
4. I .... this advertisement in a newspaper yesterday.
5. She .... her shoes and put them in a bag before crossing the waterlogged street.
6. He was .... by his grandparents.
7. We must ...., or we will miss the train.
8. As I tried to pick up the bucket, its handle ....

GRAMMAR

Main and Subordinate Clauses

- A **clause** is a group of words containing a subject and a predicate with a finite verb.
  - A **main clause** expresses a complete idea by itself. It is also called an **independent clause**. It can stand as a sentence on its own. For example:

    I am visiting China next week.

- A **subordinate clause** cannot stand as a sentence on its own. It is also known as a **dependent clause**. It begins with a subordinating conjunction or a relative pronoun. For example:

  Before you leave for home, please give me a call.
  (subordinate clause) (main clause)

A. Underline each clause in the sentences and say whether it is a main clause (MC) or a subordinate clause (SC).

1. I could not meet her as she was not home. [ ]
2. I will wait for you until you return. [ ]
3. We left early so that we could arrive on time. [ ]
4. I don't know whether he will accept my offer. [ ]
5. If you eat junk food often, you will become obese. [ ]
6. I am sure that he will help me. [ ]
7. The teacher said that honesty is the best policy. [ ]
8. Do you know where Lina lives? [ ]
9. The man who stole my laptop has been arrested. [ ]
10. It is difficult to say how many candidates will pass the test. [ ]
11. I first met him when I lived in Indore. [ ]
12. The train had left before I reached the station. [ ]

Coordinating and Subordinating Conjunctions

- **Coordinating conjunctions** are used to join one main clause to another. For example:

  I invited him to my birthday party, but he didn't come.

- Coordinating conjunctions are *and, but, or, nor, for, yet,* and *so.*
- **Subordinating conjunctions** are used to join a dependent clause to a main clause. For example:

  I could not call you as I was busy.

  Here are some common subordinating conjunctions:

after rather than since so that than that though unless although
as because before even if even though if in order that until
when whenever where whereas wherever whether while

B. **Underline the conjunction in each sentence and say whether it is a coordinating conjunction (CC) or a subordinating conjunction (SC).**

1. It is so hot that I am sweating constantly.
2. She laughed when the puppy chased its tail.
3. I tried to contact Sasha, but she didn't pick up the phone.
4. Whoever comes first in the race will win a trophy.
5. Cut the sheet of paper in half before you decorate it.
6. Water the plants regularly, or they will die.
7. It was very hot, so I stayed at home.
8. Although he is sixty, he is quite strong.
9. I didn't tease him, nor did I eat his lunch.
10. Do you know if he wants to participate in the race?

LISTENING AND SPEAKING

Listening

A. **Listen carefully and match the sentence parts in column A with those in column B.**

Column A	Column B
1. In the 19th century,	a. also assists in the advancement of women.
2. In 1946,	b. the women's rights movement began.
3. The UNESCO	c. denied the women the right to work at night.
4. The 'protective' legislation	d. the UN set up a special commission to study the status of women worldwide.

Speaking

B. **Work in pairs and take turns to ask and answer these questions about women's rights. You can also ask questions of your own.**

1. What do you understand by women's rights?
2. What impact does it have on society if women enjoy the same rights as men?
3. What are organisations like the UN and UNESCO doing to ensure that women have their rights?

WRITING

Write an email to your school principal requesting him/her to allow you to participate in a drawing competition to be held in a neighbouring school. Say what the competition is all about and why you want to participate in it.

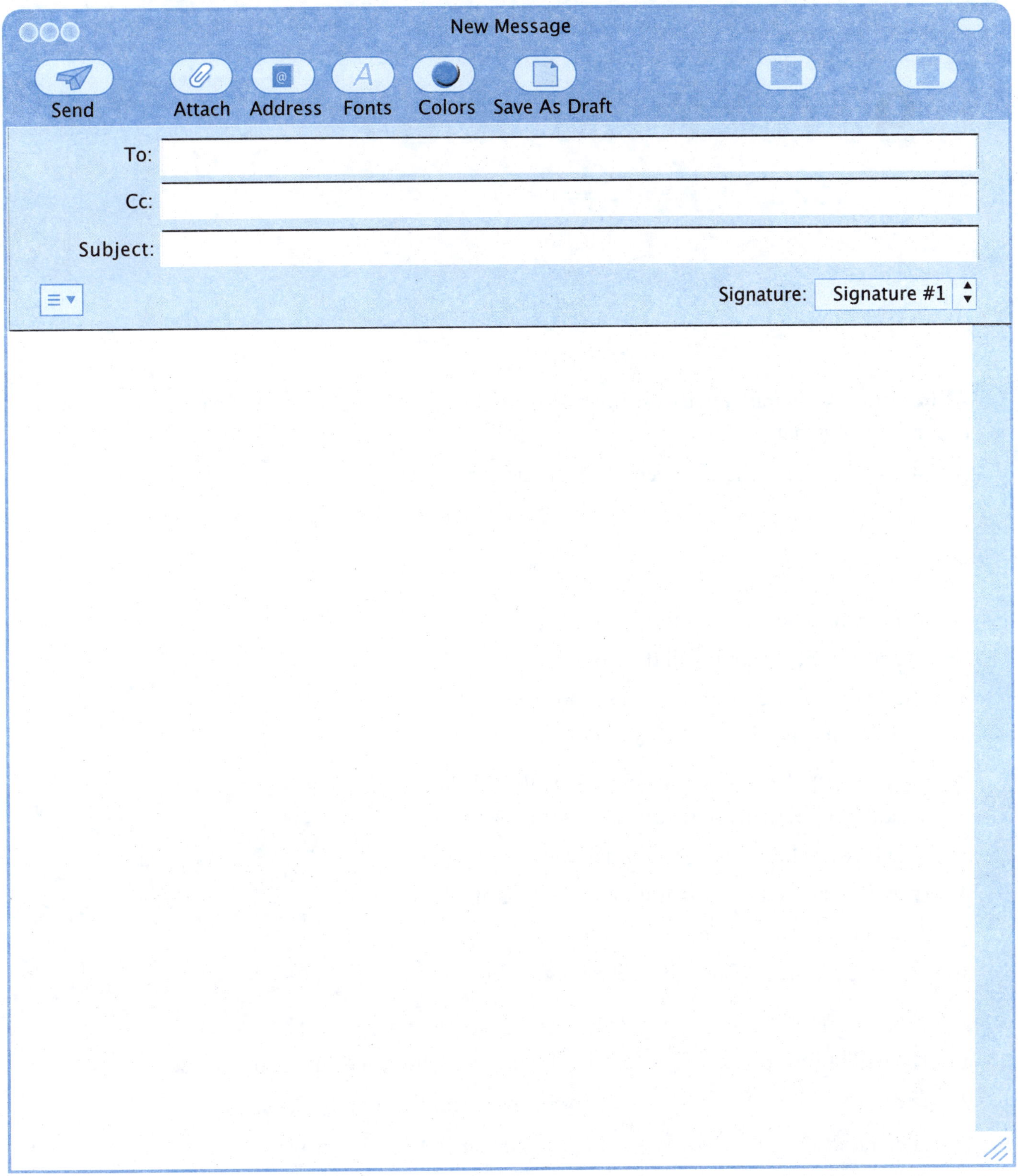

9 The Way Through the Woods

VOCABULARY

Alliteration

- **Alliteration** is a literary device in which a series of words having the same first consonant sound occur close together.
- Alliteration is usually used in poems, songs, and tongue twisters. For example:

  Kim kept kicking the ball.

A. Read the sentences and underline the consonant sounds that produce alliteration.

1. Harry Smith hated humming.
2. Arvind's aunt ate apples all the time.
3. The animal allegedly attacked a schoolboy.
4. Harry's cat clawed his couch all night.
5. Deepa enjoys watching English films while eating.
6. Mukul bought many matching ties at the market.
7. Lina loves lychees, mangoes, and grapes.
8. Walter wondered if Wally was angry with him.
9. Some people play games and practise dance in the park.
10. Ganesh's giraffe gobbled gooseberries greedily.

B. Fill in each blank with a word that helps create alliteration in the sentence.

1. The ball bounced .... to the backyard of my house.
2. The .... couldn't control the men in the cabin.
3. The grass .... greener in the olive grove.

4. Tom's .... has hard hooves.
5. The red .... were wrapped in ribbons.
6. David did not ...., nor did he sing.
7. Neeta's nephew needs .... pens.
8. The little boy bought .... flowers for his sister.
9. Latika .... the lamp at night.
10. The principal .... the paper plane made by Raman.

C. **Fill in the blanks with words from the box to create alliteration in the sentences.**

took	*niece*	*whistled*	*stood*	*noisy*	*snake*

1. My neighbours are not normally ....
2. Nancy nabbed her .... by the nape of her neck.
3. The .... slithered across the sandy seaside.
4. The store clerk .... up and stared at me.
5. The teacher .... away the troublemakers' toys.
6. The wind .... through the weeping willows.

Imagery

- **Imagery** is language that creates pictures of objects, actions, and ideas in the minds of readers or listeners.
- It appeals to our sense.

For example, these lines from William Wordsworth's poem *Daffodils* create images of floating clouds and daffodils in our minds:

I wandered lonely as a cloud
That floats on high o'er vales and hills,
When all at once I saw a crowd,
A host, of golden daffodils;
Beside the lake, beneath the trees,
Fluttering and dancing in the breeze.

D. **These sentences contain imagery. Say briefly what picture appears before your mind's eye as you read them and what senses each sentence mainly appeals to.**

1. 'The woods are lovely, dark and deep,/But I have promises to keep.'

....

....

2. 'And full-grown lambs loud bleat from hilly bourn;/Hedge-crickets sing'

....

....

3. The children were screaming and shouting in the fields.

....

....

4. He breathed in the aroma of brewed coffee.

....

....

5. The girl ran her hands over the soft satin fabric.

....

....

WRITING

A. Arrange the panels of the comic strip in correct order.

B. Write appropriate dialogue in each speech bubble to create a comic strip that shows people ordering food at a restaurant.

TEST 3 (20 marks)

VOCABULARY .... (5)

Write two antonyms for each of these words.

1. isolated ....
2. filthy ....
3. messy ....
4. impure ....
5. deserted ....

GRAMMAR .... (10)

A. Underline the main clause and the subordinate clause in each sentence. We have done the first one for you. **(5)**

She did this *<u>because she wished so.</u>*

(main clause) (subordinate clause)

1. Just as she reached Paris, rain began to fall.
2. The Police asked her many questions when she came back to her room.
3. If you drink too much you may fall sick.
4. I often wonder how you are getting on with your sister.
5. I live in the same city where you were born. (Adjective clause)

B. Punctuate the sentences below by inserting hyphens and dashes **(5)**

1. He is the recipient of the third highest gallantry award in army.
2. Will you apply for reexamination of your papers?
3. Are you sure the Police has sent the body for post mortem?
4. The telephone company is trying to enhance the user experience with its value added services.
5. What is the computer generated password for this application?

WRITING .... (5)

Imagine you want to do travel to Andaman Islands. Now you write an email to the tour operator making a couple of queries. First, state the purpose of your email, and then, as you make queries provide, some background information to each query.

10 The Ransom of Red Chief

READING

Read this story about a man's experience with his friends at a country house.

An Uncomfortable Bed

One autumn I went to stay for the hunting season with some friends in a chateau in Picardy. My friends were fond of practical joking.

When I arrived, they gave me a princely reception, which at once aroused distrust in my heart. We had some excellent shooting. They embraced me, they cajoled me, as if they expected to have great fun at my expense. I said to myself: 'Look out, old man! They have something in preparation for you.'

During the dinner, the mirth was excessive, far too great, in fact. I thought: 'Here are people who take a double share of amusement, and apparently without reason. They must be looking out in their own minds for some good bit of fun. Assuredly I am to be the victim of the joke. Attention!'

During the entire evening, everyone laughed in an exaggerated fashion. I smelled a practical joke in the air. But what was it? I was watchful, restless. I did not let a word or a meaning, or a gesture escape me. Everyone seemed to me an object of suspicion, and I even looked distrustfully at the faces of the servants.

The hour rang for going to bed, and the whole household came to escort me to my room. Why? They called to me, 'Good night.' I entered the apartment, shut the door, and remained standing, without moving a single step, holding the wax candle in my hand. I heard laughter and whispering in the corridor. Without doubt, they were spying on me. I cast a glance around the walls, the furniture, the ceiling, the hangings, the floor. I saw nothing to justify my suspicion. I heard persons moving about outside my door. I had no doubt they were looking through the keyhole.

An idea came to my head: 'My candle may suddenly go out, and leave me in darkness.' I went across to the mantelpiece and lighted all the wax candles that were on it. After that, I cast another glance around me without discovering anything. I advanced with short steps, carefully examining the apartment. Nothing. I inspected every article one after the other. Still nothing. I went over to the window. The shutters, large wooden shutters, were open. I shut them with great care, and then drew the curtains, enormous velvet curtains, and I placed a chair in front of them, so as to have nothing to fear from without.

Then I cautiously sat down. The armchair was solid. I did not venture to get into the bed. However, time was flying, and I came to the conclusion that I was being ridiculous. If they were spying on me, as I supposed, they must, while waiting for the success of the joke they had been preparing for me, have been laughing enormously at my terror. So I made up my mind to go to bed. But the bed was particularly suspicious-looking. I pulled at the curtains. They seemed to be secure. All the same, there was danger. I was going perhaps to receive a cold shower from overhead, or perhaps, the moment I stretched myself out, to find myself sinking under the floor with my mattress. I searched in my memory for all the practical jokes of which I ever had experience. And I did not want to be caught. Ah! Certainly not! Certainly not! Then I suddenly came to think of a precaution which I consider one of extreme efficacy: I caught hold of the side of the mattress gingerly, and very slowly drew it towards me. It came away, followed by the sheet and the rest of the bedclothes. I dragged all these objects into the very middle of the room, facing the entrance door. I made my bed over again as best I could. Then, I extinguished all the candles, and, groping my way, I slipped under the bedclothes.

For at least another hour, I remained awake, starting at the slightest sound. Everything seemed quiet in the chateau. I fell asleep.

I must have been in a deep sleep for a long time, but all of a sudden, I was awakened with a start by the fall of a heavy body tumbling right on top of my own body, and, at the same time, I received on my face, on my neck, and on my chest, a burning liquid which made me utter a howl of pain. And a dreadful noise, as if a sideboard laden with plates and dishes had fallen down, penetrated my ears. I felt myself suffocating under the weight that was crushing me and preventing me from moving. I stretched out my hand to find out what was the nature of this object. I felt a face, a nose, and whiskers. Then with all my strength, I launched out a blow over this face. But I immediately received a hail of cuffings, which made me jump straight out of the soaked sheets, and rush in my nightshirt into the corridor, the door of which I found open.

O stupor! It was broad daylight. The noise brought my friends hurrying into the apartment, and we found, sprawling over my improvised bed, the dismayed valet, who, while bringing me my morning cup of tea, had tripped over this obstacle in the middle of the floor, and fallen on his stomach, spilling, in spite of himself, my breakfast over my face.

The precautions I had taken in closing the shutters and going to sleep in the middle of the room had only brought about the interlude I had been striving to avoid.

Ah! How they all laughed that day!

– Guy de Maupassant

COMPREHENSION

A. Fill in the blanks with correct words.

1. The author says his friends were fond of .... joking.
2. They gave the author a princely .... on his arrival.
3. During the entire evening, everyone .... in an exaggerated fashion.
4. The author shut the .... with great care and then drew the curtains.

B. Answer the questions in brief.

1. Where did the author go? What season was it?
2. 'Look out, old man! They have something in preparation for you.' Why did the author say that to himself?
3. What made the author sense a practical joke in the air in the evening?
4. How was the author awakened from his sleep?
5. Find antonyms of these words in the story.
   a. calm: ....
   b. carelessly: ....

C. Think and answer the questions.

1. Did the precautions taken by the author work well for him? Explain.
2. Do you find the story funny? Give reasons for your answer.

3. If you were in the author's place, would you be equally suspicious of your friends' behaviour? Justify your answer.

....

....

....

VOCABULARY

A. Choose the correct word for each definition.

1. One who loves one's country: .... (*patriot/charioteer/defender*)
2. One who goes to settle in another country: .... (*foreigner/native/emigrant*)
3. Intentional damage caused to equipment, transport or public property: .... (*calamity/sabotage/movement*)
4. One who loves mankind: .... (*philosopher/agnostic/philanthropist*)
5. One who is new to something and has little experience in it: .... (*litigant/novice/plaintiff*)
6. A structure made for workers to stand on when they are working on a building: .... (*scaffold/rafter/staircase*)
7. A style that uses more words than required: .... (*verbose/pedantic/rhetorical*)
8. An official who lives in a foreign country as a representative of his/her own country: .... (*secretary/ambassador/advocate*)
9. Written by an unknown author: .... (*pseudonym/anonymous/alias*)
10. One who looks at the brighter side of things: .... (*pessimist/optician/optimist*)

Portmanteau Words

Portmanteau words are words formed by joining parts of two different words together, usually combining their meanings. For example:

brunch (breakfast + lunch) *motel (motorcar + hotel)*

B. Write the words from which these portmanteau words have been formed. You can take the help of a dictionary. Also, use the portmanteau words in sentences of your own.

1. chortle ....

....

2. emoticon ....

....

3. flare ....

....

4. electrocution ....

....

5. malware ....

....

6. vidiot ....

....

GRAMMAR

Direct and Indirect Speech

Study the direct and indirect speech forms.

Direct Speech	Indirect Speech
'I'm ready to go,' I said to them.	*I told them (that) I was ready to go.*
'Are you ready?' the teacher asked the students.	*The teacher asked the students if they were ready.*
'What are you doing?' he said to me.	*He asked me what I was doing.*
'Please close the door!' he said to me.	*He requested me to close the door.*
'Who are you?' the woman asked the boy.	*The woman asked the boy who he was.*
The principal said to the students, 'Open your notebooks.'	*The principal asked the students to open their notebooks.*
The woman asked the man, 'Did you see anybody take away my bag from the car?'	*The woman asked the man if he had seen anybody take away her bag from the car.*
The girl said to her father, 'Please buy me a new pair of shoes.'	*The girl requested her father to buy her a new pair of shoes.*
The gardener said to the children, 'Don't walk on the grass.'	*The gardener told the children not to walk on the grass.*

A. Rewrite the sentences in direct speech.

1. He told me that he was ill.

....

2. I asked him if he would help me.

....

3. The engineer said that he had finished the job.

....

4. The traveller asked me where the nearest bus stop was.

....

5. The patient asked the doctor if he could drink coffee.

....

6. My father advises me not to eat fast food.

....

7. She said that she worked in a bank.

....

8. Raj suggested that they should wait for Rita.

....

9. Deepa wanted to know where I had been.

....

10. Sameer told his younger sister not to waste her money on toys.

....

11. The man said that he couldn't drive a lorry.

....

12. David told me that his father was fifty years old.

....

13. Monica asked me if I wanted to dance.

....

14. Shikha and Sheeba said that they needed new phones.

....

15. The teacher asked me if my parents had arrived.

....

B. Your friend said these things to you yesterday. Rewrite the sentences using reported speech.

1. 'Manu was a brave girl.'
2. 'Ramesh is keen on working on his grammar skills.'
3. 'Pinky could not compete with Rinku.'
4. 'Tina wastes money on useless things.'
5. 'Manita wakes up early even on Sundays.'
6. 'Lina was born in Meerut.'
7. 'The children are returning from school.'
8. 'India is the world's largest democracy.'
9. 'Raman and Suman are playing in the park.'
10. 'Raghav's parents have gone out of town.'

LISTENING AND SPEAKING

Listening

A. Listen to a conversation and answer the questions.

1. What language is Raman learning?
2. How often does he have classes every week?

3. What is the duration of the class?

4. What happens when a learner uses a wrong word or sentence?

5. What funny thing does Raman say at the end?

Speaking

Extempore: Expressing an Opinion

Extempore speech is not a prepared speech. But as you speak, you should keep thinking and arranging your ideas mentally. Keep these points in mind while delivering an extempore speech.

- Start with an introductory sentence and then elaborate on it.
- Give examples to make your point clear.
- Be careful about your diction and tone.
- Maintain eye-contact with your audience.

B. Deliver an extempore speech on the topic: *Gender Inequality in Indian Society*.

C. Your teacher has asked you to suggest ways in which your school could be made more interesting for students. Deliver an extempore speech in class sharing your ideas.

WRITING

Diary entry

- **Diary writing** is a very effective and natural tool for expressing and recording our experiences, feelings, and actions without any restrictions.
- The date, day and time of writing a diary entry is usually mentioned at the beginning of the diary entry. It is frank, informal writing, so we can freely express our ideas and feelings.

You had participated in an art competition in your school today. Write a diary entry expressing your feelings about the event.

11 The Cookie Thief

VOCABULARY

Metaphor

- **Metaphor** is a figure of speech in which a comparison between two different things is made without using the words *like* or *as*.
- In a metaphor, a word is used to represent something other than its literal meaning. For example:

  Life is an empty dream. (The comparison here is made between two different things, life and dream, without using *like* or *as*. Thus, it is a metaphor.)

A. Identify the two things compared in each sentence and say what the comparison suggests.

1. The school race winner is a cheetah. ....

   ....

2. Necessity is the mother of invention. ....

   ....

3. He is the only hope of his family. ....

   ....

4. Lina is an angel; she helps everyone. ....

   ....

5. My dog is a circus clown. He always makes me laugh. ....

   ....

6. Our cricket coach says our team captain is a diamond. ....

   ....

7. My mother's call is the best medicine to cure my homesickness. ....

....

8. The wind was a wolf howling in the forest. ....

....

B. Write eight sentences of your own using metaphors.

1. ....

....

2. ....

....

3. ....

....

4. ....

....

5. ....

....

6. ....

....

7. ....

....

8. ....

....

Proverbs

A **proverb** is a short sentence or a saying that states a truth or gives a piece of advice based on common sense or experience. For example:

A bird in the hand is worth two in the bush.

A friend in need is a friend indeed.

A little learning is a dangerous thing.

A penny saved is a penny earned.

C. Match each proverb with its meaning. Then make sentences using the given proverbs.

Proverb	Meaning
1. A leopard can't change its spots.	a. If the result of something is good, it compensates for any previous difficulties or unpleasantness.
2. A rolling stone gathers no moss.	b. When an organisation or a state fails, it is the leadership that is the root cause.
3. A fish rots from the head down.	c. One who doesn't settle at any place but keeps moving, doesn't achieve much.
4. Loose lips sink ships.	d. People can't change how they are.
5. All's well that ends well.	e. Careless, unguarded talk may cause problems for one.

1. ....

....

2. ....

....

3. ....

....

4. ....

....

5. ....

....

D. Explain the meaning of each proverb in your own words. You may take the help of a dictionary.

1. When in Rome, do as the Romans do. ....

....

2. Two wrongs don't make a right. ....

....

3. To err is human, to forgive divine. ....

....

4. Charity begins at home. ....

....

5. Power corrupts; absolute power corrupts absolutely. ....

....

E. **Say which proverb expresses each situation.**

You can't have your cake and eat it too.
Beggars can't be choosers.
If you can't beat them, join them.

1. You don't like watching films, but your friends love that. You tell your friends not to waste time watching films and play outdoor games instead; but they don't listen to you and insist that you join them. Finally, you agree to watch a film with them.

   ....

2. You apply for a four days' leave to attend your cousin's wedding but you are granted only two days' leave. You have no choice but to accept it.

   ....

3. You are at a shop with your friend to buy a backpack as you're going on a trip. There is only one bag that you like, but it is very expensive. You don't want to spend so much on a bag as you want to save as much money for the trip as possible.

   ....

WRITING

Limerick

A **limerick** is a well-known poetic form. It is a humorous poem consisting of five lines with a bouncy rhythm.

The pattern and form of a limerick is as follows:

- It has five lines.
- Lines 1, 2, and 5 rhyme with one another.
- Lines 3 and 4 rhyme with each other.

Look at this limerick by Edward Lear.

There was a young lady whose bonnet,
Came untied when the birds sate upon it;
But she said: 'I don't care!
All the birds in the air
Are welcome to sit on my bonnet!'

The last words of lines 1, 2 and 5 (*bonnet, it,* and *bonnet*) rhyme. The last words of lines 3 and 4, *care* and *air*, also rhyme.

Write a limerick on a subject of your choice. When you have completed the limerick, check to see if the rhyme scheme follows that of a limerick. If not, rewrite some words to correct the rhyme scheme.

TEST 4

(20 marks)

VOCABULARY ....(5)

Match the proverbs with its correct meanings.

Proverbs	Meanings
1. All's well that ends well.	a. Make use of an opportunity immediately.
2. Barking dogs never bite.	b. You cannot rely on the situation always.
3. As you make your bed, so you must lie.	c. If everything ends in a good way, you can forget its difficult past.
4. One swallow doesn't make a summer.	d. Noisy threats often do not warn of real danger.
5. Strike while the iron is hot.	e. You must accept consequences of your act.

GRAMMAR ....(10)

A. Rewrite the statements below as reported speech **(5)**

1. 'My father gave me a bicycle,' Amol told his friends.
2. 'I won't switch off the lights until I go to bed', she said.
3. 'I haven't gone to watch a film for years', Jason told his mother.
4. 'Tanisha didn't want to study till midnight', Tarun told her friends.
5. 'Finish your homework first before you watch TV', Pankaj said to his sister.

B. Fill in the gaps with a conjunction from the list below. **(5)**

whether	*although*	*but*	*while*	*because*

1. She did tell me about it .... I couldn't respond due to illness.
2. Trisha was late in office .... the car didn't pick up her up on time.
3. He couldn't survive ....he received the best possible medical care.
4. .... I was reading a story in the bus, it crossed my destination.
5. Do you know .... she has left India?

WRITING (5)

Write a limerick rhyming lines 1,2,5 and lines 3 and 4.

12 Raymond's Run

READING

Read this article about Manish Singh Rawat, an Indian race walker.

Manish Singh Rawat: The Unsung Hero of the Rio Olympics

Though the Rio Olympics in 2016 gave India new sporting icons, several heartening stories of Indian players went unnoticed in the race for medals. Few people know that India was represented by a part-time waiter at the race-walking event at the Rio Olympics. Fewer still know that he bested the previous Olympic medal winners in the competition and narrowly missed the bronze medal by less than a minute's difference. This is the inspiring story of Manish Singh Rawat, who went from selling tea and working in the fields to fulfilling his dream of taking part in the Olympics.

In 2002, when Manish Rawat's father passed away, the ten-year-old boy saw his mother toil in the fields to make ends meet for her family of four children, including him. Rawat would work with his mother on the farm in the morning before heading to school, about seven kilometre away by foot. In 2006, he took up a part-time job as a waiter at a small eatery near his hometown, Sattar, in the Chamoli district of Uttarakhand. With two sisters and a young brother at home, Rawat had a hard time sustaining his family on his meagre income as a waiter. Knowing that excelling in athletics could help him get a government job, Rawat decided to pursue race walking.

Race walking is a long-distance discipline within athletics. Although it is a foot race, it is different from running because here, one foot must appear to be in contact with the ground at all times over the course of 20 km. This is why apart from the inherent stamina, technique and fitness required in any long-distance race, race walking also tests mental focus.

In an interview, Rawat said: 'I won't mind admitting this, but race walking has a rather funny posture. So people do end up laughing. But the funny posture exists for a reason because the feet have to be planted on the ground. So when I used to run in my village, people used to laugh at me.'

But Rawat refused to be put off by the lack of world-class equipment and a stream of naysayers at Badrinath who would make fun of his walking practice. Training on the hilly terrain in torn shoes, Rawat continued to juggle several jobs to make ends meet for his family and also support his training. From working as a house help and tourist guide to labouring on farms and driving tractors, the Uttarakhand lad did everything.

In 2010, Rawat tried to get a job with the police but he was rejected. This was financially the most difficult time for him, and Rawat considered quitting the sport to support his family. It was his coach who convinced Rawat that he was making good progress and that he had a future in the sport.

Manish finally made the cut in the 20-km event after finishing with a time of 1:20:50 at the IAAF Race Walking Challenge in April 2015. His 3:57:11 effort at the World Championship in Beijing also earned him a Rio berth for the 50-km race-walking event. For the Rio Olympics, the 25-year-old Rawat trained under the Russian coach Alexander Artsybashev in the national camp at Ooty with other race walkers.

Having reached the finals of the 20-km event at Rio, Rawat finished 13th, ahead of some of the best race walkers in the world, including 4 former world champions, 3 Asian champions, 2 European champions and even 2 Olympic medalists. He registered a final timing of 1:21:21, less than a minute behind the bronze medalist. But this incredible achievement against the best in the world was missed by the mainstream media.

Race walking is considered to be a less important sport in India. But ever since Kerala's KT Irfan finished 10th at the London Olympics, the country has produced four Asian champions. For the Rio Olympics, as many as nine race walkers qualified and three had to be dropped because India didn't have enough spots.

India's national race-walking team coach, Alexander Artsybashev, believes that the sport has great possibilities in the country if the Indian authorities take it more seriously. Top medal-winning countries at the Olympics spend millions of dollars to produce one champion—the UK recently declared that it spent 5.5 million pounds on each medal winner. On the other hand, in India, champions in the making fight unenviable battles all the time, just like Rawat. And yet, their raw talent and determination to defy all odds to fight their way to the top is no less than amazing. It's time that athletes like Rawat, who will soon start training again to participate in the 2020 Tokyo Olympics in the hope of winning a medal, get the backing and respect they deserve.

– Sanchari Pal

COMPREHENSION

A. Mark the statements as true (T) or false (F).

1. Manish Rawat is a race walker from the Chamoli district of Uttarakhand. ☐
2. Manish Rawat comes from a poor family. ☐

3. His father passed away when Manish Rawat was twenty years old. ☐
4. Manish Rawat became a police officer in 2006. ☐
5. At the Rio Olympics, Manish Rawat finished thirteenth, ahead of some of the best race walkers in the world. ☐

B. Answer the questions in brief.

1. How far was Rawat's school from his house?

....

....

....

2. What is race walking? How is it different from other races?

....

....

....

3. What qualities does an athlete need for race walking?

....

....

....

4. How did Manish Rawat perform at the World Championship in Beijing?

....

....

....

....

5. How did he perform at the Rio Olympics?

....

....

....

....

6. Find synonyms of these words in the passage.

a. encouraging .... b. accepting ....

c. difficulties .... d. unbelievable ....

C. Think and answer the questions.

1. What does Alexander Artsybashev think about India's future in race walking? Do you agree with him?

2. How is Indian race walkers' journey to big international events different from that of their competitors from countries like the UK? What can be done to bridge the gap?

VOCABULARY

Prefixes

In English, we often form negative words by adding negative prefixes to nouns, adjectives, and verbs. Some common negative prefixes in English are *il-*, *im-*, *in-*, *ir-*, *dis-*. For example:

indigestion *irreparable* *invisible*

A. Form negative words by adding the above prefixes to these words. Then use the new words in sentences of your own.

1. ....possible: ....
2. ....legal: ....
3. ....mount: ....
4. ....literate: ....
5. ....accurate: ....
6. ....organic: ....
7. ....mobile: ....
8. ....sane: ....
9. ....reconcilable: ....
10. ....eligible: ....

11. ....moral: ....

12. ....perfect: ....

13. ....comfort: ....

14. ....consistent: ....

15. ....coherent: ....

Suffixes

Suffixes are letters or groups of letters added to the end of words to form new words. For example:

improvement *stagnation*

B. Form abstract nouns by adding the suffixes *-tion, -ment, -ness,* and *-al* to the words. Then use them in sentences of your own.

1. fond .... : ....
....
2. replace .... : ....
....
3. arrive .... : ....
....
4. judge .... : ....
....
5. refuse .... : ....
....
6. create .... : ....
....
7. survive .... : ....
....
8. reduce .... : ....
....
9. govern .... : ....
....
10. adjust .... : ....
....
11. achieve .... : ....
....

12. recognise .... : ....

13. bitter .... : ....

14. combine .... : ....

15. dismiss .... : ....

GRAMMAR

Simple, Compound and Complex Sentences

- A **simple sentence** has only one clause. For example:

  He is a doctor.

- A **compound sentence** consists of two or more independent clauses. A coordinating conjunction such as *and, but, for, so, yet, or,* or *nor* is used to join independent clauses to form compound sentences. For example:

  He gave me a storybook, and I gave him a diary.

- A **complex sentence** consists of one independent/main clause and one or more dependent clauses. The clauses are joined with a subordinating conjunction like *that, if, unless, though, after, before, as, because, although* or *since,* or with a word like *who, which, why, where, when* or *how*. For example:

  If you don't have a pen, you can take mine.

A. Make changes in the sentences as instructed. One has been done for you.

1. You are right. I think so. (Join the sentences with *that*.)

   I think that you are right.

2. Raju did not complete his work. He went to sleep early. (Join the sentences with *but*.)

   ....

3. Rohan was scared of being left alone in the house. He started crying. (Join the sentences with *and*.)

   ....

4. Sunil is the fastest runner in the school. He doesn't want to participate in this race. (Join the sentences with *but*.)

   ....

5. Arjun is a good speaker. He is a little shy. (Join the sentences with *though.*)

....

6. The play ended. The audience clapped immediately after. (Join the sentences with *as soon as.*)

....

7. Lina is a great artist. I know that. (Join the sentences with *that.*)

....

8. It was very hot outside. I stayed at home. (Join the sentences with *so.*)

....

9. He has complained to the police. They are looking into the matter. (Join the sentences with *and.*)

....

10. He was skilled in painting. He was not allowed to participate in the painting competition. (Join the sentences with *yet.*)

....

B. Rewrite the sentences as directed.

1. He tried his best, but he didn't succeed. (*complex sentence*)

....

2. The clown entered the circus ring, and the children started clapping. (*complex sentence*)

....

3. If you take care of small things, big things will take care of themselves. (*compound sentence*)

....

4. You must hurry, or you will miss the bus. (*complex sentence*)

....

5. The battle has been won, but the war isn't over yet. (*complex sentence*)

....

6. Ria decorated the cookies that Piyush made. (*compound sentence*)

....

7. You have to be minimum eighteen years old to be eligible to vote. (*complex sentence*)

....

8. Leprosy is curable, and everybody knows this. (*complex sentence*)

....

9. He is a magician from Turkey who has performed all over the world. (*compound sentence*)

....

10. Neither the colour nor the design of this dress appeals to me. (*compound sentence*)

....

Conditional Clauses

- Conditional sentences have a main clause and a **conditional clause** (sometimes called an if-clause).
- The conditional clause usually begins with *if* or *unless*. It can come before or after the main clause. For example:

  If you eat junk food, you will become obese.

- There are different types of conditional sentence.
- When expressing a future event or action, the main clause uses *will, can, may,* or *might* + the base form of a main verb. The if-clause uses the simple present tense. For example:

  If Rohit comes to me, I will certainly help him.

  These type of sentences suggest that the action in the main clause is quite likely to take place.

- When referring to something that is always true if the condition is met, both the clauses use the simple present tense. For example:

  If I do not know the meaning of a word, I always look it up in a dictionary.

- When a sentence expresses an imaginary situation, the main clause uses *would, could,* or *might* + the base form of a main verb. The if-clause uses the simple past tense. For example:

  If you found a lot of diamonds, what would you do?

C. Fill in each blank with the correct form of the verb. Also, use *will/would* with the verb wherever necessary.

1. If I were an astronaut, I .... (*travel*) to Mars.
2. If she .... (*study*) hard, she will pass the exam with good grades.
3. If you don't handle the box carefully, the cups .... (*break*).
4. If I had magic powers, I .... (*make*) everyone in the world happy.
5. If he switches on the button, what .... (*happen*)?
6. How would you behave with the common people if you .... (*become*) a powerful politician?

LISTENING AND SPEAKING

Listening

A. Listen carefully and fill in the blanks.

1. A university must do more than provide a .... apprenticeship.
2. Every student must be educated to become a good, ... person.
3. Students should learn to observe restraint so that restraints do not have to be ....

4. Human .... cannot be escaped on the grounds of being a scientist or technologist.
5. Students should be able to think clearly and .... so that false doctrines do not gain ground.

Speaking

B. You want to be a journalist. You have been offered an internship by a national newspaper. If you accept the offer, you will need to work from 3:00 p.m. to 7:00 p.m. on Fridays, Saturdays and Sundays. Then, you will be unable to attend your sports classes on Fridays and Saturdays. Work with a partner, who will play your sports teacher, and discuss the matter with him/her, trying to find a solution.

WRITING

A. How are smartphones affecting our life? Write a short article on the disadvantages of using a smartphone too much.

....

....

....

....

....

....

....

....

....

....

....

....

....

....

....

....

B. Have you ever done something for a stranger? Narrate the incident in the form of a diary entry.

13 Prayer of a Sportsman

VOCABULARY

A. Match each sports idiom to its meaning. Then use any three in sentences of your own.

Idiom	Meaning
1. To jump the gun	a. a mere guess
2. A shot in the dark	b. equal or the same for everyone
3. To throw in the towel	c. to achieve an easy victory
4. Across the board	d. to act prematurely, especially without thinking carefully about it
5. To go overboard	e. to give up
6. To win hands down	f. to become too excited about something

Palindromes

- A **palindrome** is a word, phrase, or sentence that reads the same backwards and forwards.
- The word *palindrome* has been derived from the Greek word *palindromos*, which means *running back again*. For example:

  race car   *my gym*   *Now I won.*

- *Tattarrattat* is the longest palindrome in English. It was coined by the famous novelist James Joyce in *Ulysses*, referring to *a knock on the door.*

B. Read these definitions and write the palindromes they refer to.

Definition	Palindrome
1. A system that detects the movement of planes, ships, and missiles	
2. A language spoken in Kerala	
3. 12 o'clock in the middle of the day	
4. Officially related to a town or city	
5. The raised part at the back end of a ship	
6. A thing that rotates or causes something to rotate	

C. Complete these palindromes and write their meanings.

1. ref.......... : ....
2. lev.......... : ....
3. pe......... : ....
4. ten.......... : ....
5. de......... : ....

WRITING

Advertisement

All businesses, campaigns, drives and social events need promotion. We can promote a business, a campaign, or an event through effective advertising. Effective advertising helps a business or product to reach out to a lot of people. To create an effective **advertisement**, we need to think carefully about what will persuade people best and make them take the message seriously.

In a business advertisement, we need to convince our potential customers why our business should be their number one choice, and why they shouldn't even consider our competitors. This is commonly referred to as the unique selling proposition (USP).

This means our advertisement must say to our prospective customers, 'Buy this product for this specific benefit.' Catchy tag lines are used to give the message in a powerful way.

Write an advertisement for a storybook you have recently read. Include information about what makes the book unique and why people should buy it.

TEST 5

(20 marks)

VOCABULARY .... (5)

1. Add the correct negative *prefixes* to the adjectives. Then, write them in the blanks.

1. perfect, ...
2. literate ....
3. regular ....
4. tidy ....
5. mature ....

GRAMMAR .... (10)

A. Change the sentences as directed. **(5)**

1. Nora admitted that he had forged her father's signature. (Simple sentence)
2. Only meritorious student can pass this test. (Complex sentence)
3. He was poor, but he was honest in his dealings.(Simple sentence)
4. Besides being intelligent, she is beautiful. (Compound sentence)
5. Although there is lockdown, the spread of infection has increased. (Simple sentence

B. Match 1-5 to a-e to make sentences **(5)**

1. If you multiply two by zero.	a. which charges fees.
2. When it rains	b. you get zero.
3. Children won't go to school	c. he will get the job.
4. If he doesn't accept the offer	d. if he doesn't clear all semesters.
5. Ramesh will not get the degree	e. we don't play in the ground

WRITING .... (5)

Write a review of an advertisement that you have seen recently. Include general information about the advertisement such as its title, genre etc. Summarize your opinion about it. Try to conclude the review in an interesting way.

....

....

14 Sonam Wangchuk

READING

Read this poem on pollution and the harm it causes to the environment.

Warned

The sands of time have rendered fear
Blue skies on high no longer clear
Stars were bright whence they came
Now dimmed, obscured, pollution's haze.

Crystal clear our waters gleamed
Fish abundant, rivers streamed
Ocean floors sandy white
Now littered, brown, pollution's plight.

Trees towered high above
Trunks baring professed love
Birds chirping from sites unseen
Gone, paper joined pollution's team.

One can't blame pollution alone
As they say, you reap what you've sown
So let us plant a better seed
Tear our old roots, cultivate, weed.

Protect what has been given for free
Our waters, skies, wildlife and trees
For once they're gone, don't you say
Consider yourself warned of that fatal day.

– *Sylvia Stults*

COMPREHENSION

A. Read the lines from the poem and answer the questions.

1. *Crystal clear our waters gleamed*
   Fish abundant, rivers streamed
   Ocean floors sandy white
   Now littered, brown, pollution's plight.

   a. How were the ocean floors in the past?

   ....

   b. What has changed things?

   ....

2. *One can't blame pollution alone*
   As they say, you reap what you've sown.

   a. What can't we blame alone for the sad situation?

   ....

   b. What does 'you reap what you've sown' mean?

   ....

B. Answer the questions in brief.

1. What is the theme of the poem?

   ....

   ....

2. Why are the blue skies no longer clear?

   ....

   ....

3. How does the poet describe trees?

   ....

   ....

4. 'Tear our old roots, cultivate, weed.' Explain this line.

   ....

   ....

5. What has been given for free? Why do we need to protect it and how?

   ....

   ....

C. Think and answer the questions.

1. How has paper joined *pollution's team*? Explain.

....

....

....

2. What does the poet mean by planting a *better seed*? How can that be done?

....

....

....

3. Do you think the title of the poem is appropriate? Justify your answer.

....

....

....

VOCABULARY

Neologisms

The English language is evolving constantly and new words, terms, and phrases are being added to it continuously. These new words and phrases are regularly used in oral communication, but they are not yet accepted in the mainstream language. Such words and expressions are called **neologisms.** Neologisms may also be words that have acquired meanings that are different from their original meanings. For example:

selfie *google*

A. Match each neologism to its meaning correctly. Then use any three in sentences of your own.

Neologism	Meaning
1. staycation	a. an application for a smartphone or a computer
2. troll	b. the activity of getting a group of people to contribute to a task
3. app	c. repeated status updates about one's location in an attempt to get attention
4. crowdsourcing	d. an individual who posts insulting, rude, and obnoxious comments online
5. geobragging	e. a vacation at home or in the immediate local area
6. noob	f. someone new to an online community or game

Homophones

Homophones are similar-sounding words. They have different spellings and meanings but the same pronunciation. For example:

idle – idol *compliment – complement* *farther – father*

B. Make sentences with these homophones to show the difference in their meanings.

1. a. stationary: ....

   b. stationery: ....

2. a. principle: ....

   b. principal: ....

3. a. advise: ....

   b. advice: ....

4. a. bear: ....

   b. bare: ....

5. a. aisle: ....

   b. isle: ....

6. a. loose: ....

   ....

   b. lose: ....

   ....

7. a. accept: ....

   ....

   b. except: ....

   ....

8. a. allowed: ....

   ....

   b. aloud: ....

   ....

9. a. coarse: ....

   ....

   b. course: ....

   ....

10. a. mayor: ....

   ....

   b. mare: ....

   ....

C. Fill in the blanks with the correct words from the almost similar sounding words.

1. He was arrested for engaging in .... (*illicit/elicit*) activities.
2. I took his comment about my performance as a .... (*complement/compliment*).
3. The children collected .... (*cells/shells*) on the beach.
4. The .... (*principal/principle*) addressed the morning assembly yesterday.
5. Laser photography gives an .... (*allusion/illusion*) of reality.
6. She achieved success in .... (*adverse/averse*) circumstances.
7. She .... (*apprised/appraised*) us of the situation.
8. She is famous for her wit as well as her .... (*simple/sample*) style.
9. How will this policy change .... (*affect/effect*) you?
10. He .... (*effected/affected*) a stunning goal.

Homonyms and Homographs

- **Homonyms** are words which have the same spelling and pronunciation but different meanings. For example:

  bill: the hard, pointed part of a bird's mouth

  bill: a written statement of the money to be paid for something

- **Homographs** are words that are spelt the same but have different pronunciations and meanings.

  minute: (pronounced like *mi.nit*) a duration of sixty seconds

  minute: (pronounced like *my.nyoot*) extremely small or very detailed

D. Make two sentences using each pair of homonyms.

1. a. engaged: ....

   b. engaged: ....

2. a. crane: ....

   b. crane: ....

3. a. foil: ....

   b. foil: ....

4. a. net: ....

   b. net: ....

5. a. date: ....

   b. date: ....

6. a. right: ....

   b. right: ....

7. a. band: ....

....

b. band: ....

....

8. a. tire: ....

....

b. tire: ....

....

9. a. lie: ....

....

b. lie: ....

....

10. a. rose: ....

....

b. rose: ....

....

GRAMMAR

Active and Passive Voice

- A sentence is usually written in the **active voice** or the **passive voice**.
- In the active voice, the subject performs the action expressed by the verb in the sentence. For example:

  Shefali changed the tablecloth.
- In the passive voice, the subject is acted upon and the doer of the action comes after the verb. For example:

  The tablecloth was changed by Shefali.

A. Change the voice in the sentences.

1. Raju was praised by the teacher.

....

2. That famous scientist is known to me.

....

3. Your mother taught us mathematics.

....

4. Mamta drew a picture showing life in the city.

....

5. We all know the facts.

....

6. A century was scored by Virat Kohli yesterday.

....

7. By whom was our national anthem written?

....

8. The wounded soldier was being helped by an old woman.

....

9. Nazia drank the bitter medicine in one gulp.

....

10. The old man gave toffees to all the children in the playground.

....

11. Ranjana made some special tea for everyone.

....

12. The court rejected his appeal.

....

13. The strike has been called off by the employees.

....

14. Those living in glass houses should not throw stones at others.

....

15. The students will write an application to the principal.

....

Defining and Non-defining Clauses

- A **defining clause** is a clause that explains which person or thing we are talking about. It is necessary to identify the person or thing. There is no comma before a defining clause. For example:

  The diary that has a red cover is mine.
  The principal awarded the boy who played the prince in the play.

- A **non-defining clause** is a clause that gives extra information about a person or thing. It is not necessary to help us understand which person or thing is being talked about. There is always a comma before a non-defining clause, and one after it if the sentence continues. For example:

  Mumbai, which is the capital of Maharashtra, is a metro city.
  Dr S. Radhakrishnan, who was India's second president, was a great thinker.

B. Underline the defining and non-defining clauses in these sentences. Write *D* for defining clause and *ND* for non-defining clause.

1. The film that we saw last week was awful. ☐
2. That's the town where he comes from. ☐
3. John's guitar, which he bought in the sixties, still works fine. ☐
4. I gave my dictionary to Prakash, who is my close friend. ☐
5. Have you read the novel that you bought last week? ☐
6. Ann, whom I admire, is not right in this case. ☐
7. Do you know the children who are playing outside? ☐
8. This is the village where my father was born. ☐

LISTENING AND SPEAKING

Listening

A. Listen carefully and fill in the blanks.

1. The Sahara is the world's largest .... desert.
2. Strong winds blowing in the Sahara often cause ....
3. Half of the Sahara receives less than an inch of .... per year.
4. Except for the ...., all the rivers and streams flowing through the Sahara are irregular or seasonal.
5. Central Sahara has very little ....

Speaking

B. Work in pairs and interview the Minister for Child Development (to be played by your partner) about the measures being taken by his/her department to solve the problem of child labour in India. Also, ask questions about the department's future plans to tackle the problem.

C. Work in groups. You are the sports captain of your school hockey team. Some of your schoolmates are complaining to you because they were not selected for the hockey team to represent the school in an upcoming inter-school hockey tournament. Speak to them, justifying the selection process and encouraging them to be optimistic about their selection in the future. You can also give them some tips on how they can improve their performance in the sport.

Pronunciation

Hard and soft *c* sounds

- In English, the letter *c* is pronounced as /k/ when followed by *a, o, u,* or a consonant, or at the end of a word. This is called the **hard c**. For example:

  cast *coat* *copper* *cut* *acute* *accurate*

- When *c* comes directly before the letter *e* , *i*, or *y*, we pronounce it as /s/. This is called the **soft c**. For example:

  city *cent* *certain* *cymbal*

D. Now practise pronouncing these words. Write /k/ or /s/ corresponding to the sound of *c* in the words.

1. celebrate ______
2. peace ______
3. coalition ______
4. accomplish ______
5. recall ______
6. fancy ______
7. recede ______
8. curtain ______
9. cyclone ______
10. icy ______

WRITING

A. Imagine you study at a boarding school. The food served at the school canteen is often too spicy. Write a letter to your school principal complaining about the problem. Mention in the letter that you and your roommates have already complained to the canteen chef and the hostel warden once, but no action was taken.

The Principal

....(*Name of the school*)

....(*Address*)

....

....(*Date*)

Subject: ....

Dear Sir/Madam, (*Salutation*)

....

....

....

....

.... (*Subscription*)

....

.... (*Your name and class*)

B. Write a letter to the editor of a local newspaper expressing your views on the problem of global warming and suggest the ways to prevent it.

The Editor

.... (*Name of the newspaper*)

.... (*Address*)

....

.... (*Date*)

Subject: ....

Sir/Madam, (*Salutation*)

....

....

....

....

....

....

....

....

....

....

....

....

....

....

....

....

....

....

Yours truly (*Subscription*)

....

.... (*Your name and address*)

15 Mother Nature's Treasures

VOCABULARY

Idioms

An **idiom** is a group of words whose meaning is different from the meanings of the individual words that form it. For example:

a change of heart: a change in one's attitude towards something

A. Match each plant idiom with its meaning.

Idiom	Meaning
1. Barking up the wrong tree	a. to mislead somebody
2. To not let the grass grow under one's feet	b. to offer a reconciliation
3. To hold out an olive branch	c. to go to bed
4. A needle in a haystack	d. something almost impossible to find
5. To lead somebody up the garden path	e. misunderstanding something
6. To hit the hay	f. to not delay in getting things done

B. Now use each idiom from exercise A in a sentence of your own.

1. ....

....

2. ....

....

3. ....

....

4. ....

....

5. ....

....

6. ....

....

C. Fill in each blank with the correct idiom. Don't forget to use the correct tense of the verbs.

a rule of thumb	*lose heart*	*add fuel to the fire*	*alive and kicking*	*grasp the nettle*

1. He was already angry and your sarcastic remark ....
2. When nobody in his family could deal with the difficult problem, he ....
3. Traditional pop music is still .... in many parts of the world.
4. As ...., we should avoid the usage of too many abbreviations in a formal writing.
5. If we fail to achieve something in our first attempt, we should not .... but keep trying until we succeed.

WRITING

Text Messages and Tweets

Sending a **text message** on the mobile phone is a quick and effective way of communication. You can use abbreviations to keep your messages short, and emoticons to express your feelings unless it is a formal message. For example:

> We can meet tmrw at Chandni Chowk Metro Station at 5 p.m. We can then visit the shops together. Ravi ☺

A. Now write a short text message to your friend to inform him that you cannot attend his birthday party because you have suddenly fallen ill. Remember to apologise and wish your friend a happy birthday. You may also use emoticons.

....

....

....

A **tweet** is a means of expressing your thoughts, feelings, and ideas on an online social platform and to the wider community. A tweet has 280 characters only, so you need to be precise and clear in your tweet. Here is a sample tweet.

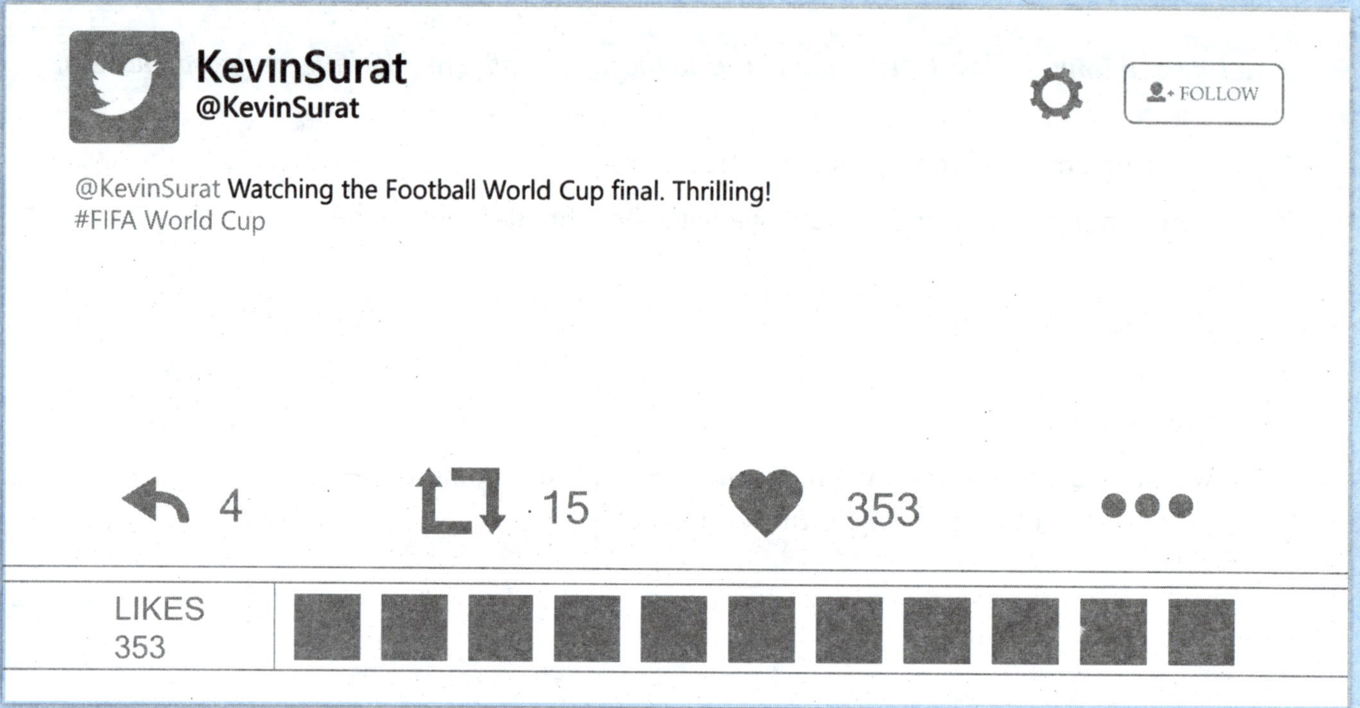

B. Write a tweet announcing a forest conservation conference in your city. Do not exceed 280 characters.

TEST 6

(20 marks)

VOCABULARY .... (5)

Choose the correct words to complete the sentences.

1. He turned .... (*pail/pale*) after suffering from jaundice for a couple of weeks.
2. The cabin crew were walking down the .... (*aisle/isle*) to serve food and drinks to the passengers in the flight.
3. I would like to receive your .... (*male/mail*) electronically.
4. The Police searched everywhere to .... (*fined/find*) the fugitive.
5. The baker stopped baking after he ran out of .... (*flour/flower*).

GRAMMAR .... (10)

A. Complete the sentences with the active or passive form of the verbs in brackets. **(5)**

1. The alarm clock .... (invent) by Levi Hutchins in 1787.
2. Another American, Walter Hunt .... (invent) the safety pin in 1849.
3. The first toothbrushes .... (make) by the Chinese in 1498.
4. Where .... the computers .... (make) today? They are mostly .... (make) in China.
5. Today many newspapers are available n the web, and only a few .... (print).

B. Underline the non-defining clause in each sentence **(5)**

1. Tigers, which are large and found in Sunderbans, are called Royal Bengal Tigers.
2. Jagat's father, who lives in Australia, has three granddaughters.
3. My colleague Sashi, who went to the same university as me, has just published a chapter in a book.
4. We stopped at the Rastrapati Bhavan, which we had never visited before.
5. She gave me the letter, which was in a white envelope. (non-defining clause)

WRITING .... (5)

You are the captain of your school cricket team. Recently you have come back from a tour of England which you joined as a member of the under sixteen national cricket team. Now write a letter to the editor of a newspaper, in which you are interested to publish your experiences of the tour. Include information about your everyday routine, weather, people, food, language. Give your opinion about the tour: what you liked and disliked.